THEOLOGY OF SEVENTH-DAY ADVENTISM

Herbert S. Bird

The value of this new study of Seventh-day Adventism is that it focusses on the *theology* of this remarkably active and growing religious fellowship. It sets forth the fundamental beliefs of Seventh-day Adventism and compares and contrasts them with the teachings of the Bible and the doctrines long held by the Christian Church. Thus the reader is led into a basic understanding and critique of this popular movement.

The book opens with a fine survey of the historical roots of Seventh-day Adventism, and then proceeds to discuss the Adventist view of the Bible, Man, Christ, Salvation, the Sabbath, and Christian Conduct. In the final chapter the author relates Seventh-day Adventism to the evangelical faith so as to avoid the extremes of a narrow sectarian at̲t̲i̲t̲u̲d̲e̲ ̲a̲n̲d̲ ̲o̲f̲ a broad liberal a̲t̲ cates the very real̲ tween Seventh-day ̲ the Christian ev̲ and points the wa̲ unity.

D1264123

Theology of
SEVENTH-DAY ADVENTISM

Theology of
Seventh-Day Adventism

by Herbert S. Bird

Christian Missionary in Eritrea
American Evangelical Mission

Wm. B. Eerdmans Publishing Company
Grand Rapids, Michigan

Contents

5

ACKNOWLEDGEMENTS

Occasionally I have borrowed words from an article of mine that will appear in Volume I of *Encyclopedia of Christianity*, to be published by Mr. Jay Green, and these are here used with his permission.

Quotations from *Testimonies for the Church* by Ellen G. White appear by permission of Ellen G. White Publications; those from *Seventh-Day Adventists Answer Questions on Doctrine, Yearbook of the Seventh-day Adventist Denomination, Bible Readings for the Home Circle, God Speaks to Modern Man* by Arthur E. Lickey, *The Prophetic Faith of Our Fathers* by Leroy E. Froom, *Drama of the Ages* by W. H. Branson, and *The Desire of Ages* and *The Great Controversy between Christ and Satan*, both by Ellen G.White, appear by permission of Review and Herald Publishing Association.

Quotations from *Body and Soul* by D. R. G. Owen appear by permission of The Westminster Press, and those from *The Epistle to the Hebrews* by B. F. Westcott by permission of Macmillan and St. Martin's Press.   — H. S. B.

This book is dedicated to
My Father and Mother

INTRODUCTION

THOUGH BARELY A CENTURY OLD, SEVENTH-DAY ADVENTISM is now one of the significant movements on the religious scene. Beginning its organized existence in 1860, this church, by virtue of a prodigious missionary enterprise, has enjoyed such steady growth that it is now a world-wide fellowship of more than a million communicants gathered into some twelve thousand churches. A recent yearbook reported forty-two denominational publishing houses producing literature in over two hundred languages. The movement also sponsors five thousand elementary and advanced schools, including a theological seminary and a medical college.

The subject of Seventh-day Adventism has never wanted for discussion. A fairly large body of literature, including both refutation by its critics and exposition and defense by its exponents, already exists, and new material continues to appear. This, however, does not make a further appraisal of this movement unnecessary, particularly since the large majority of treatments of the Seventh-day Adventist position, in the view of the writer, suffer from one of two deficiencies, both of which derive from the theological commitment of their authors. The first is common to writers who represent liberal or mediating Protestantism; for such, Seventh-day Adventism is an "oddity," to be condemned for "employing a weapon of fear to the minds of simple or superstitious people."[1] These tend to score it for its "literalism," and not infrequently treat it with something approaching contempt for what they consider to be its Biblically oriented supernaturalism.

A second deficiency is common to the large quantity of discussions of Seventh-day Adventism that proceed from the evangelical wing of Protestantism. Such writings, to be sure, frequently contain material of substantial usefulness in assessing certain features of Seventh-day Adventist doctrine. Nevertheless, most of these fall short of a satisfactory estimate of this movement to the degree that they consider "legalism" to be equivalent to a

1. James Black, *New Forms of the Old Faith* (London: Thomas Nelson and Sons, 1948), pp. 204, 207 *et passim*.

7

high view of the moral law as a standard of conduct for the Christian in this age, and condemn Seventh-day Adventism for affirming the perpetual and universal validity of the Ten Commandments.[2] It is for this reason, as well as in the hope that he may make some contribution to the discussion of this subject currently taking place in evangelical circles, that the writer offers an evaluation of Seventh-day Adventism which differs in some important respects from either of the foregoing types of treatment.

This volume has been written mainly to elucidate and give an appraisal of certain distinctive tenets of this church. Its main interest will therefore be in the theology of this movement rather than in its history or program. But if it is difficult to judge adequately *any* system of doctrine without attending to the historical circumstances in which it originated, it is impossible to do so in the case of Seventh-day Adventism. The reason for this will become clear as we proceed. Thus a summary historical survey is appropriate, and it is here that our study shall begin.

2. As Dudley M. Canright, *Seventh-day Adventism Renounced*; E. B. Jones, *Free Indeed*; Louis M. Talbot, *What's Wrong with Seventh-day Adventism?* and numerous others.

CHAPTER ONE

SEVENTH-DAY ADVENTISM AND ITS HISTORICAL ROOTS

LATE IN THE SECOND DECADE OF THE NINETEENTH CENTURY, one William Miller, a farmer and sometime soldier from the town of Low Hampton, New York, having been converted from deism to orthodox Christianity, began to apply himself to the study of the Scriptures. His independent frame of spirit exceeded only by his ambition, he allowed himself the use of the English Bible and *Cruden's Concordance,* and nothing more, in pursuing the goal of harmonizing all the apparent contradictions in Holy Writ. After two years of what seems to have been the most diligent kind of effort, Miller came to feel that he had entered into possession of a vitally important principle of interpretation. Let his own words, written to a friend and later published, tell this story:

> I laid by all commentaries, former views and prepossessions, and determined to read and try to understand for myself. I then began the reading of the Bible in a methodical manner; and by comparing scripture with scripture, and taking notice of the manner of prophesying and how it was fulfilled, I found that prophecy had been literally fulfilled. . . . I found, on a close and careful examination of the Scriptures, that God had explained all the figures and metaphors in the Bible, or had given us rules for their explanation. . . . And I discovered that God had in His Word revealed *"times and seasons"*; and in every case where time had been revealed every event was accomplished as predicted . . . in the time and manner; therefore I believed all would be accomplished. . . .[1]

As the last part of the foregoing would indicate, the subject of prophecy was Miller's particular interest. In general, he

1. J. V. Himes, *Views of the Prophecies and Prophetic Chronology Selected from Manuscripts of William Miller* (Boston: J. V. Himes, 1842), p. 12.

was persuaded that conditions in his own day, when compared with the Scriptural descriptions of "the last days," justified the view that the end was not far off. This opinion, innocuous enough in itself, all too early blossomed into the dangerous idea that by the application of certain principles of prophetic inter-pretation he could arrive at a date for the return of Christ and the judgment of the world. The details of the methods by which Miller arrived at his conclusions need not concern us here; the Seventh-day Adventist writer Nichol, however, rightly says that his first and greatest emphasis was "on the prophetic declaration, 'unto two thousand and three hundred days; then shall the sanctuary be cleansed.' Daniel 8:14."[2] The key to this prophecy was, for Miller, the "day-year" principle; thus the 2300 days meant 2300 years. Miller, by referring to Daniel 9:25, understood the beginning of this period to be the decree of Artaxerxes authorizing the return of the captive Jews to Jerusalem, issued in 457 B.C. The problem, of course, was to determine which sanctuary Daniel had in mind when he wrote, "then shall the sanctuary be cleansed." Miller's decision was that the several possibilities for the interpretation of this word, when tested by the requirements of the case, narrowed down to two, namely, the earth and the church.

Given these principles, the conclusion of the matter could not have remained very long out of reach; thus the year 1818 did not pass before Miller became settled in the conviction that another twenty-five years would see the end of the present age.

Miller did not make haste to publish his findings; he lived quietly for about nine years, sharing his discovery only with his relatives and most intimate friends. Beginning in 1831, however, by which time he had entered the Baptist ministry, he heeded the call to preach these tidings, and from then on the Advent message gained adherents with astonishing rapidity. Virtually every evangelical denomination in the United States was repre-sented in the number of his followers, the clergy not excepted. In attempting to account for this widespread interest, one must not overlook the fact that the setting of dates by the use of prophetic chronologies was by no means an innovation of William Miller's. An exhaustive study of these developments by

2. Francis D. Nichol, *The Midnight Cry* (Washington, D. C.: Review and Herald Publishing Association, 1945), p. 33.

a Seventh-day Adventist theological professor[3] is conclusive in showing that many expositors of Scripture from various denominational backgrounds had proceeded in much the same manner. (The venerable and judicious J. A. Bengel, author of the celebrated *Gnomon of the New Testament,* was one of this number; he was of the opinion that the Millennium would begin in 1836.) With few exceptions, however, those who did so expound the prophetic Word regarded some event other than the return of Christ — such as the beginning of a moral reformation in the world, the overthrow of the Turks, or the return of the Jews to Palestine — as lying at the end of the 2300 years. But none of the others found himself able to fire the popular imagination with anything that even approached the success of William Miller.

The nature of the case makes it impossible to determine, or even to give an approximation of, the number of people who accounted themselves adherents of this view. For one thing, no new churches were formed until the "Millerite"[4] phase of the Adventist movement had all but passed, nor were the names of those who assented to this teaching ever recorded. Again, "Many of those who gathered to hear the Millerites came from curiosity. . . . Others merely enjoyed the show. . . ."[5] Contemporary records, however, lend plausibility to the remark made in a Methodist periodical in 1843 that Millerism was affecting the whole public mind of New England. The same thing might have been said of western New York, where the leaders directed their attention in 1843, and where by the summer of 1844 camp meetings with attendances numbering thousands were held at such points as Cooperstown, Rochester and Buffalo (Miller himself appeared at these), as well as in many of the smaller communities across the state. There is also evidence that the doctrine had penetrated into other areas of the United States and even into other continents.

Millerism passed through several phases in the months between March 21, 1843 (the first day of the Jewish year during

3. Leroy E. Froom, *The Prophetic Faith of Our Fathers* (Washington, D. C.: Review and Herald, 1946-54), IV, 382-410.

4. "They had been known up to . . . [1844] only as Millerites. The editor of *The Advent Herald* explained that . . . the most exact title . . . would be Adventists." Nichol, *op. cit.,* pp. 206f.

5. W. R. Cross, *The Burned-over District* (Ithaca, New York: The Cornell University Press, 1950), p. 298.

which, according to Miller's calculations, the return of Christ could be expected) and October 22, 1844, the date of the "Great Disappointment." Nothing need detain us here beyond a notice concerning the latter date, which is of great significance in view of later developments. This was not chosen by Miller himself, but by another Adventist leader, one Samuel H. Snow. His view was that Christ, the antitypical High Priest, would come out of the heavenly holy of holies, where He had been ministering, on the antitypical Day of Atonement. This meant that the Second Advent of Christ would occur on the tenth day of the seventh month of the Jewish calendar, or October 21/22, 1844.[6] If there is any doubt that this view became the definitive Adventist position, there is none whatsoever that it was the theory in terms of which the majority of the faithful expected the accuracy of the predictions to be confirmed. These, assembling in numerous meeting places on the appointed day, prepared for the coming of the Lord. It should be remarked here that Nichol's *The Midnight Cry* not only affords an interesting and generally reliable account of the rise and progress of the "Millerite" movement, but demolishes effectively the rumors of widespread fanaticism among Adventist adherents, ascension robes and all, which for many years were accepted popularly as sober fact.

Inevitably, the uneventful passing of the final date, called in Adventist writings the "Great Disappointment," entailed grievous frustration for those who had committed themselves to Millerism. It would not have required a superior understanding of human nature for an observer to have predicted that if disappointed on October 22, 1844, the Millerites would suffer ridicule for a time, become divided among themselves, and at last dwindle to virtual oblivion. This almost happened. The post-Disappointment history of Millerism was, first, a wholesale sloughing off of the majority, composed of "the lukewarm, the partially interested, and guilt-conscious ones who had feared the judgment day for excellent reasons."[7] As for the convinced Adventists, there was the agonizing problem of what

6. Readers who may be interested in the somewhat involved mathematics by which Snow arrived at this date are invited to consult Froom, *op. cit.*, p. 799.

7. Cross, *op. cit.*, p. 309.

had gone wrong. Explanations abounded, but none of them proved saitsfactory in the face of the stark realities of the discrepancy between Adventism's prophetic principles and the continuation of earthly history. William Miller himself, before his death in 1849, though unable to comprehend wherein his calculations had been erroneous, and though fully expecting the return of Christ at any time, repudiated all the "new theories" which were proposed to explain what had happened. He remained a Calvinistic Baptist to the last, and never accepted the Sabbatarian view, or the "soul sleep" and annihilationist doctrines which were being introduced among the Adventists in those days. He even went so far as to declare that the "seventh-month" movement — Snow's position — was in no sense a fulfillment of prophecy.

But Millerism refused to follow the historical pattern which might have been expected for a movement of this type, and the "Great Disappointment" had hardly passed before an episode occurred which led directly to the founding of the Seventh-day Adventist denomination. The time was early in the morning of October 23, 1844, and the place a corn field in Port Gibson, New York, where the leader of the Adventists of that district, Hiram Edson, had gone walking, pondering as he went the failure of Christ to return to earth as scheduled. It was just then, according to his later testimony, that he was granted a wonderful vision, the substance of which was that the sanctuary which was to be cleansed was not an earthly sanctuary at all, but the antitypical holy of holies in heaven. In other words, the calculations of the Adventists, at least of those who held the "seventh-month" position, were correct. October 22, 1844, had indeed been the end of a prophetic period. It was not in their arithmetic but only in their understanding of the event which was to take place that the Millerites had been wrong. Since this has important implications for the development of Seventh-day Adventist doctrine, it is well that Edson's own account of his vision be cited. According to Loughborough, a contemporary of Edson's and a chronicler of early Adventist history, Edson declared:

> . . . that instead of our High Priest *coming out* of the Most Holy of the heavenly sanctuary to come to this earth on the tenth day of the seventh month, at the end of the

2300 days, he for the first time *entered* on that day the second apartment of that sanctuary, and that he had a work to perform in the Most Holy before coming to this earth.[8]

Intensive study in ensuing months by Edson and certain Adventist associates served to reinforce the conviction that here was the key to the entire problem, and before long this view was being circulated widely among the Adventists.

It was at about this time that another development took place which was to contribute a second distinctive feature to this branch of the Adventist movement. This was the introduction of Sabbatarianism, which was accomplished at a conference of Adventist leaders at Edson's place. The prime mover here was Joseph Bates of New Bedford, Massachussetts. A Millerite follower, Bates, if not a Seventh Day Baptist, was one with them at least on the question of the Sabbath, and when he came into contact with those who were studying the "sanctuary position" he addressed himself particularly to the matter of the relationship of these two teachings. The other Adventists seem not to have required much convincing; Edson in particular found Bates's presentation of his position most delightful, and as he concluded arose and declared, "That is light and truth. The seventh day is the Sabbath, and I am with you to keep it!"[9]

But the foundations of Seventh-day Adventist doctrine were not yet complete. One more element, lacking which it may be doubted that the movement would have flourished to the degree that it has, was necessary. This is what is referred to as the "Spirit of prophecy," by which the church soon to be born would not only enjoy counsel and direction, but would possess an authoritative witness to the correctness of its interpretation of the message of the Bible. The human agent through whom this endowment came was Ellen Gould Harmon, later Mrs. James White, of Portland, Maine. Ellen as a young woman had been a Millerite follower; in fact, it is likely that the lectures of William Miller himself, given in Portland, had influenced her and her parents to such a degree that they were led to embrace the Adventist faith. For this aberration they were "dis-

8. Quoted in Froom, *op. cit.*, p. 881.
9. Quoted in Froom, *op. cit.*, p. 904.

fellowshipped" from the Methodist Church in 1842. (The holding of Adventist doctrine was, after a time, considered grounds for disciplinary action by some Protestant churches.) At the time of the "Great Disappointment," Ellen Harmon, then seventeen years old, was among those who had come to regard the "seventh-month" movement as mistaken. In December, 1844, however, while in prayer with some other women of Adventist faith, she experienced her first vision:

> While we were praying, the power of God came upon me as I had never felt it before. I seemed to be surrounded with light, and to be rising higher and higher from the earth. At this time I had a view of the experience of the advent believers, the coming of Christ, and the reward to be given to the faithful.[10]

This became for Ellen Harmon and her companions a vindication of the seventh-month position. Vindication, however, was not the most important result of this mystical experience; Ellen soon became convinced that she had received a gracious bestowal of the gift of prophecy. "An unspeakable awe filled me," she wrote later, "that I, so young and feeble, should be chosen as the instrument by which God would give light to His people."[11] Thus it became her cherished conviction that from then on it was given to her to hear directly the voice of God. Since the Portland group and the Sabbatarian Adventists, represented by Edson and Bates, were both part of the same original movement and mutually acquainted, it was only a short while before they entered into correspondence and discussion. The precise order of developments is not known, but the upshot was that over the course of a few years the Whites (Ellen Harmon and James White, a prominent Adventist worker, were married in 1846) accepted Sabbatarianism and the sanctuary teaching, and Bates and his group became convinced that Mrs. White was indeed a messenger of light to the people of God. How important this was to the doctrinal and organizational development of Seventh-day Adventism can be surmised from the

10. Ellen G. White, *Testimonies for the Church* (Mountain View, California: The Pacific Press, 1882-1909, 9 volumes in 4), V, 654f.
11. *Ibid.*, I, 62.

following extract from Froom's account of a meeting at Volney, New York, on August 18, 1848:

> There was much diversity of view . . . [which] occasioned much serious prayer and study. Mrs. White was shown some of their errors in contrast to the opposite truths. She was bidden to admonish the contenders to yield their errors. . . . To this they responded, and the discordant elements were brought into harmony.[12]

Needless to say, the possession of such a gift as this made for a wonderful unanimity.

The Sabbatarian Adventists, as they came to be called, continued their conferences over a period of years. In 1860 formal organization was accomplished, and the name *The Seventh-day Adventist Church* adopted. Early in the denomination's history certain other distinctive views joined the "foundational doctrines" as part of the message which it considers to be "present truth." Among these were the ideas of conditional immortality and annihilationism, neither of which is original with nor peculiar to Seventh-day Adventism. Premillennialism, albeit of a discrete variety, also appeared. A further point which developed more gradually is concerned with the "message of the third angel" (Rev. 14:9ff.); this involves a schematization of the events of the end times which is, as far as this writer knows, the private property of this movement.

In addition to these doctrinal features, Seventh-day Adventism has always given a place of major emphasis to what it calls "health reform." This is accounted for by the fact that Mrs. White, early in her career as the organ of the "Spirit of prophecy," received the impression that she was called to give counsels to God's people concerning the care of the body. A large proportion of her voluminous writings, therefore, is concerned with the care of the sick, etc., and the denomination has for many years implemented this teaching by maintaining hospitals, rest homes and the like in many countries. Members of the church, in accordance with her instructions, are required to abstain from all flesh foods which the Old Testament pronounces unclean. Many Seventh-day Adventists, moreover, following a recommended

12. Froom, *op. cit.*, p. 1022.

health measure, partake of no flesh foods at all, although this is
not mandatory.

As we turn from Seventh-day Adventism's origins to scrutinize
its main doctrines, the procedure will be to discuss in turn those
teachings which are either peculiar to itself or sufficiently distinctive to warrant inclusion in this study.   Seventh-day Adventists, to be sure, are not the only "Adventists"; several other
groups share Millerism as their fountainhead and have more or
fewer points in common with the church established by Mrs.
White and her associates.   Here, however, since Seventh-day
Adventism alone is to come under discussion, we shall use the
various forms of the terms "Seventh-day Adventism" and "Adventism" interchangeably with reference to this church or its
system of doctrine.

CHAPTER TWO

SEVENTH-DAY ADVENTISM AND THE WORD OF GOD

BASIC TO THE STUDY OF ANY MOVEMENT WITHIN THE GENERAL
Christian tradition is the question of authority; what is its rule
of faith and life? Is its belief and practice informed by the
Bible alone, by something else, or by a combination of the two?
The answer to such questions is of particular importance in the
case of Seventh-day Adventism, for here the church's principal
teacher occupies a place which has no parallel among organizations within the pale of Protestantism; Mrs. White is no mere
founder of the denomination or formulator of its creed. It
shall, therefore, be the intent of the present chapter to define
Seventh-day Adventism's view of the work, especially of the
literary efforts, of Ellen G. White, and to attempt to determine
what this position implies for the doctrine of the Word of God.

MRS. WHITE'S EXPERIENCE AND WRITINGS

As far as is known, the first intimation that Ellen Harmon ever
had that hers was to be a place of unique service in the Adventist
cause was at the time of her first vision, the details of which have
already been cited. Others followed shortly. In "Testimony
Number Thirty-three"[1] she gives an account of the second of
these; this was the vision which contained her commission
to relate to others what God had shown to her. It is therefore
of special importance for our purposes here. Among other
things, she wrote this concerning it:

1. *Testimonies for the Church* is a nine volume work consisting of thirty-
seven groups of articles and essays on various doctrinal and practical
subjects. It includes such titles as "Parental Responsibility," "Fanaticism
in Wisconsin," "The Word Made Flesh," and "Healthful Cookery."
"Testimony Number Thirty-three" is concerned with Mrs. White's writings
as such. It is largely a series of extracts from her other "Testimonies"
which bear upon the visions and the place of her writings within the
framework of divine revelation.

> In a second vision . . . I was shown the trials through
> which I must pass, and that it was my duty to go and relate
> to others what God had revealed to me. . . . The teaching
> of this vision troubled me exceedingly, for it pointed out
> my duty to go out among the people and present the truth.
> . . . It was a great cross for me to relate to the erring what
> had been shown me concerning them. . . . And when obliged
> to declare the messages I would often soften them down. . . .
> I did not realize the danger and sin of such a course until
> I was taken into the presence of Jesus. He looked upon me
> with a frown. . . . With this solemn warning before me I
> went out to speak to the people the words of reproof and
> instruction given me of God.[2]

The foregoing leaves no room for doubt that Mrs. White
considered herself to have received special revelations from
God. The very heavens were opened to her view, and she
held discourse with both angelic dignitaries and the glorified
Jesus. Her task, to which she admitted an instinctive distaste,
was to deliver such instruction as she received to the individuals
or groups for whom they were intended, or to the church at
large. How often was she favoured with visitations of this type?
According to her husband, she had from one to two hundred such
experiences in the course of twenty-three years.[3] These served
the purpose both of advising and warning the Adventist people
and of strengthening their conviction that their distinctive views
were correct. Many of the visions which were directed to
individual members of the movement were written out for
them at their request; a number of these appeared later in print.
The reason for the publication of such material, we are informed,
was in order that those who did not receive an individual
communication might not consider themselves to be in no need
of counsel or rebuke.

Mrs. White's published writings are voluminous, consisting of
over twenty thousand pages of book manuscript and some three
thousand periodical articles.[4] These, however, are neither

---

2. White, *op. cit.*, V, 654ff.
3. See Francis D. Nichol, *Ellen G. White and Her Critics* (Washington, D. C.: Review and Herald, 1951), p. 52.
4. Froom, *op. cit.*, lists her published works (IV, 1235-1237).

entirely nor primarily records of her visions. Indeed, it would appear that as the years passed the number of these "open visions" decreased, and the messages which she received came either through the medium of dreams or through some manner of influence on her mind during her waking hours.[5]

It may be regarded as established, then, that Ellen White conceived of herself as an instrument of direct divine revelation. It is equally certain that there were some among the Seventh-day Adventists, especially in the earlier years, who were not convinced that the visions and other manifestations of the gift of prophecy were of divine origin and thus binding upon their consciences. She wrote, for example, that "those who are reproved by the Spirit of God should not rise up against the humble instrument. It is God and not an erring mortal who has spoken to save them from ruin."[6] But answers such as this led quite logically to a further difficulty; some at least from among her followers concluded that this was nothing if it was not a claim that here were writings in a class with the books of the Bible, and thus an addition to the canon of Holy Scripture. We find, therefore, that Mrs. White felt it necessary to reply to the charge of certain critics, who were evidently right within the Adventist ranks, that the *Testimonies* were an addition to the Word of God:

> Brother R. would confuse the mind by making it appear that the light God has given through the *Testimonies* is an addition to the Word of God; but in this he presents the matter in a false light. God has seen fit in this manner to bring the minds of His people to His Word, to give them a clearer understanding of it. The Word of God is sufficient to enlighten the most beclouded mind, and may be understood by those who have any desire to understand it. But notwithstanding all this, some who profess to make the Word of God their study are found living in

5. See James E. Bear, "The Bible and Modern Religions," 1. "The Seventh-day Adventists." *Interpretation*, X, 1 (1956), p. 66.

6. White, *op. cit.*, III, 257. Another of similar import reads: "In ancient times God spoke to men by the mouth of prophets and apostles. In these days He speaks to them by the testimonies of His Spirit. There was never a time when God instructed His people more earnestly than He instructs them now concerning His will and the course He would have them pursue." (*Ibid.*, V, 663).

direct opposition to its plainest teachings. Then, to leave
man without excuse, God gives plain and pointed testimonies, bringing them back to the Word that they have
neglected to follow.[7]

It seems reasonable, therefore, to conclude from this that
Ellen White regarded the visions, and evidently the entire body
of her writings, as manifestations of the "Spirit of prophecy,"
long denied to the church but now restored. These, being messages from God Himself, were fully authoritative for those to
whom they were addressed. In her thinking, however, *they were
not to be considered an addition to the canon of Holy Scripture.*
Their place was subordinate to the Bible as an aid to the understanding and application of its teachings. In Mrs. White's
words, they were "a lesser light to lead men and women to the
greater light [the Bible]."[8]

SEVENTH-DAY ADVENTISM'S VIEW OF MRS. WHITE'S WORK

The restoration of the prophetic gift was, as we have seen,
one of the foundational principles of the Seventh-day Adventist
movement. It stands to reason, therefore, that general agreement on this point having been attained, there would from that
time forward be little room for difference of opinion concerning
it, at least among the spokesmen for the denomination.[9] However, both by way of developing their own doctrines and answering questions which continued to appear, it became necessary
for the leaders of this movement, as time passed, to expound
the matter more fully. The official statements of doctrine are
somewhat lacking in depth — this is due, no doubt, to the
tendency in Seventh-day Adventism to disparage creedal formulations.[10] Sufficient material of a semi-official character, how-

---

7. White, *op. cit.,* V, 661.

8. White, "An Open Letter" (1903), quoted by Froom, *op. cit.,* p. 975.

9. It may be noted that the Seventh-day Adventist Church insists that
it does not make the writings of Mrs. White a test of fellowship. There
is no reason to doubt that this is true. Having once embraced Adventism, however, one would be unlikely to deny the authority of these
writings without renouncing most or all of the other distinctive tenets.
Moreover, anyone in the church who questioned this point would not be
permitted to propagandize for his views; he would thus be distinctly a
"second class" member.

10. See *Seventh-day Adventists Answer Questions on Doctrine* (Washington, D. C.: Review and Herald, 1957), pp. 29, 31.

ever, has been produced to shed some light upon the details of this tenet as it is understood by the Adventists, and to answer certain questions which would occur to a reader of the denomination's official declarations.

One place where we may presume that we have the official word of the church is in its twenty-two page statement, "Fundamental Beliefs of Seventh-day Adventists," which appears in each number of its yearbook and elsewhere as well. The section on the subject of the "Spirit of prophecy" reads:

> 19. [Adventists believe] that God has placed in His church the gifts of the Holy Spirit, as enumerated in 1 Corinthians 12 and Ephesians 4. That these gifts operate in harmony with the divine principles of the Bible, and are given for the perfecting of the saints, the work of the ministry, the edifying of the body of Christ (Rev. 12:17; 19:10; 1 Cor. 1:5-7). That the gift of the Spirit of prophecy is one of the identifying marks of the remnant church (1 Cor. 1:5-7; 12:1, 28; Rev. 12:17; 19:10; Amos 3:7; Hosea 12:10, 13). They recognize that this gift was manifested in the life and ministry of Ellen G. White.

A baptismal certificate, issued to those who, upon confession of belief in the church's principles and submersion in water are received as members, contains something of like import:

> Seventh-day Adventists believe that the gift of the Spirit was early manifested among them through the work and writings of Mrs. Ellen G. White. They believe that just as in past ages God raised up prophets and messengers to perform a work for His church, and to counsel and warn God's people in time of special peril and need, so in these last days He raised up Mrs. White and bestowed upon her the gift of prophecy.

As has been remarked, these statements are not very full. Nor does the point which Seventh-day Adventism is attempting to make lie so clearly on the face of the several "proof texts" that further explanation can be dispensed with. Thus, in order to penetrate to the heart of the matter, we turn to the denomination's representative spokesmen. What, in the view of these, does Adventism understand by the manifestation of the "Spirit of prophecy" through the work and writings of Ellen G. White? The first question which arises in this connection is that of the restoration of the gift as such. Why may its latter-day appearance be expected? The discussion found in Froom's exhaustive work is typical of the denomination's apologetic at this point, and represents what is perhaps the most able defence of this position that has appeared so far. His line of reasoning is as follows:[11]

(1) In past ages the prophets were people called from many different walks of life to be spiritual guides to the people of God. These not only foretold the future but gave counsel to those of their own times. God's messages to such came in various modes: visions, dreams, oral communications and otherwise.

(2) The canonical Scriptures are the supreme gift of prophecy, "next to Christ himself, and the Holy Spirit, God's best gift to man."

(3) Prophecy is a blessing which was given to the Christian church along with other gifts of the Spirit, nor was it confined to the apostles or writers of the Bible. Appeal is made here to cases such as those of Agabus, the prophets at Antioch, Judas and Silas, and the four daughters of Philip the Evangelist.

(4) God's method of prophetic revelation was to give to the prophets the instruction which they, in turn, were to give to the people. Some of the prophetic messages were never recorded; others, as those of Gad and Jasher, were written messages but were not included in the sacred canon.

(5) The early church lost her first love "while ecclesiastical machinery multiplied and dogma crystallized into creeds." Thus the gift of prophecy faded. When the developing Catholic Church usurped authority, the pope came to be regarded as God's mouthpiece, and was eventually declared infallible when speaking officially on matters of faith and morals. Another cause which led to the elimination of the prophetic ministry was the appearance of false prophets, whose pretensions threw discredit on the genuine ones (1 Cor. 14:26-29 is cited in this connection). The fanatical "Zwickau prophets" of Reformation times were the cause of rejection by the main Protestant bodies of "any and all claims to the prophetic gift," and led to the contention that this was confined to the ages of the Old Testa-

11. This discussion may be found in Froom, *op. cit.*, pp. 964-1006.

ment and the apostles. Froom remarks in passing that the alleged revelations of such groups as the Irvingites and Mormons have often justified this attitude.

(6) The restoration of the gift of prophecy in the last days to the "remnant church" is an expectation which the Scriptures encourage. An example of Scriptural data of this type is the warning which Jesus issued against the appearance of false prophets in the days before His second coming (see Matt. 24:24). If He had not meant for His people to await the restoration of the prophetic gift He would have warned them against *all* prophets. The conclusion to which Froom feels all this must lead is that the prophetic gift was to be restored as part of God's plan for His last-day, remnant people, who would be "keepers of the commandments of God and the faith of Jesus." These would also have the "testimony of Jesus, which is defined as the Spirit of prophecy (Rev. 19:10)." Needless to say, Seventh-day Adventism is, for Froom, the "remnant church" predicted in Revelation 12:17.

So runs the argument for the expectation of the prophetic gift. But it has not yet been shown that the "Spirit of prophecy" has, in fact, appeared in the church. Hence, when it is asked, "How may it be determined that Mrs. White was a true vehicle of the Spirit?" Froom lists four "sure Biblical tests" which, he feels, she passes. These are:

(1) Conformity "to the law and to the testimony" (Isa. 8:20).

(2) Fidelity to the verities of the faith (Deut. 13:1-5).

(3) The wholesome character of the fruits it brings forth (1 John 4:1-5).

(4) The fulfillment of its predictions (Deut. 18:20-22).

Now by applying rigidly these tests of a true prophetic manifestation, Seventh-day Adventism feels that there can be no question of the right of Mrs. White to a place in the company of the chosen servants of God. Froom shows in some detail how this is so. In summary, it was found that Mrs. White was unqualifiedly faithful to the Scriptures; her writings exalt the Bible, teach obedience to all of God's commandments, and are in harmony with what former prophets taught. Secondly, her writings are true to the fundamental Christian doctrines. Again, her ministry was calculated to teach the highest ideals and to build Christian character. Finally, the fulfillment of her predictions witnesses to the genuineness of the gift.[12] Thus the denomination looks upon Mrs. White not as its founder nor as the originator of the doctrines distinctive with itself; she is, for the Adventists, "one chosen of God to help keep their feet upon the solid rock of Scripture — the true Protestant position."[13]

Ellen White, however, was by no means the last Adventist to be compelled to come to grips with the question of the relationship of the "messages" to the Bible. Thus before undertaking an examination of this entire question, we do well to determine whether the position of Mrs. White herself, discussed earlier, has seen any further developments. In their latest work on their beliefs, *Seventh-day Adventists Answer Questions on Doctrine*, which is conceived of as an accurate, though not yet "official"[14] statement of their position, they set forth these three points:

> (1) That we do not regard the writings of Ellen G. White as an addition to the sacred canon of Scripture.
>
> (2) That we do not think of them as of universal application, as is the Bible, but particularly for the Seventh-day Adventist Church.
>
> (3) That we do not regard them in the same sense as the Holy Scriptures, which stand alone and unique as the standard by which all other writings must be judged.[15]

Such is the denominational position defensively stated. Their writers maintain zealously that the Scriptures are for them the supreme standard; the messages of Mrs. White are to be regarded neither as superseding the Bible nor as the canon by which the Bible is to be tested. On the contrary, it is their contention that

---

12. Froom devotes twenty pages to an analysis of various predictions made by Mrs. White. These include "streams of published light circling the globe," the rise of spiritism, troubles and disasters for cities, the cataclysmic world wars, etc.

13. Froom, *op. cit.,* p. 972.

14. They say on page 9: ". . . because of the very nature of the Seventh-day Adventist Church organization it is impossible to consider this book as a denominationally official statement of doctrine. . . . No statement of Seventh-day Adventist belief can be considered official unless it is adopted by the General Conference in quadrennial session . . . ."

15. *Questions on Doctrine,* p. 89.

they test the writings of Mrs. White by the Bible. In defining the nature of this relationship, the Adventists make effective use of the analogy of the writers of the prophetical books which were not included in the Old or New Testaments. In spite of the fact that the literary products of these contemporaries of the writers of the Bible were never a part of the canon, these were messengers of the same God who spoke through the prophets whose works are part of Holy Scripture.

One or two additional observations are necessary. The expression, "Spirit of prophecy" looms large in Adventist discussions of these questions. This term, of course, is a direct quotation from Revelation 19:10: ". . . worship God: for the testimony of Jesus is the spirit of prophecy." The standard Adventist interpretation of this is that by "Spirit of prophecy" is meant the Holy Spirit as He speaks through a prophet of God's choosing. They understand that this gift, which was present among God's people in Old Testament times, belongs also to the final section — the remnant portion — of the Christian church.

Again, the Adventist comparison of the works of Mrs. White to a magnifying glass should be mentioned:

> [The Spirit of prophecy counsels are] an aid to a fuller, clearer understanding of the Bible . . . [to be] likened to a magnifying glass that brings out, not something new, but details that otherwise might be missed by the unaided human eye.[16]

This is urged in support of the Adventist insistence that every distinctive doctrine of their movement was derived from the study of the Scriptures: "No single major doctrine was ever initially received through the Spirit of prophecy. The doctrines were simply confirmed by the gift, or the concept broadened, or erroneous ideas pointed out."[17]

THE ADVENTIST POSITION ON THE WORD OF GOD EXAMINED

Seventh-day Adventism is committed to the historic Protestant view of the divine origin of the canonical books of the Bible. Further, it seems never to have been troubled by the presence within its ranks of any type of naturalistic higher criticism. The point at which evangelical Christianity must join issue with

16. Froom, *op. cit.,* p. 975.
17. *Ibid.,* p. 976.

the position of this movement is therefore not that of the *inspiration* of the Scriptures but that of their *sufficiency*: the *scriptura sola* principle as formulated, for example in the *Westminster Confession of Faith*, I, 6:

> The whole counsel of God, concerning all things necessary for His own glory, man's salvation, faith and life, is either expressly set down in Scripture, or by good and necessary consequence may be deduced from Scripture: unto which nothing at any time is to be added, whether by new revelations of the Spirit, or traditions of men.

A few preliminary observations are offered before this matter is taken up in detail. For one thing, in assessing the "Spirit of prophecy" teaching in Seventh-day Adventism, it is unlikely that much is to be gained by engaging, so to speak, in a quest of the historical Mrs. White. Whether, as certain anti-Adventist writings insist, she was "neurotic, fanatical, dictatorial," and "ruled [the movement] with an iron hand,"[18] or whether she was the consecrated leader and paragon of Christian virtue that Froom, Nichol and other Adventist leaders represent her as having been is a question which, for our purpose, is beside the point. Nor, in similar vein, do we accept the dilemma proposed by Mrs. White and reiterated by those who followed her for explaining the source of her messages, namely:

> My work . . . bears the stamp of God or the stamp of the enemy. There is no halfway work in the matter. The Testimonies are of the Spirit of God, or of the devil.[19]

The alternative that the writings proceeded from Mrs. White's own not inconsiderable imagination, while it admittedly lacks some of the colorfulness of the other possibilities, is certainly not to be rejected out of hand. And while complete objectivity in reading the works of so controversial a figure is doubtless impossible, even the best-intentioned non-Adventist would be likely to judge that some of her offerings are trite and picayune.

18. L. T. Talbot, *What's Wrong with Seventh-day Adventism?* (Findlay, Ohio: Dunham Publishing Company, 1956), p. 15. See also Dudley M. Canright, *Seventh-day Adventism Renounced* (Kalamazoo, Michigan, 1888), *passim*.

19. White, *Testimonies*, IV, 270. See also Froom, *op. cit.*, pp. 989ff.

There are also passages in which there is a palpable deficiency of doctrinal or historical accuracy. But banality, though assuredly a result of the Fall, is not necessarily demonic; nor for that matter is even patent error always to be ascribed to the direct influence of the pit. On the other hand, even the most vigorous critics of the Adventist movement can hardly deny that there are many things both true and relevant in Mrs. White's publications. But this is something less than to acknowledge them as communications from Heaven.

Once again, the claim of fulfilled prophecy is not of great importance: certainly true servants of God *did* make predictions which later came to pass, but this does not exclude the possibility that false prophets *might* have: Balaam's case is instructive here. And such criteria as "wholesomeness" and fidelity to the faith" suffer, after all, from the defect of assuming one of the important points at issue, namely, whether Mrs. White's views on certain controverted matters are indeed "wholesome" and faithful to Christian verities.

Thus it is to the question of the sufficiency of Holy Scripture that we now turn, giving our attention to those aspects of the doctrine which bear upon the claims of Seventh-day Adventism for Mrs. White's writings. First, the claim that the prophetic gift has reappeared deserves some scrutiny. It has been noted that the denomination insists that no additions are to be made to canonical Scripture: "Seventh-day Adventists uniformly believe that the canon of Scripture closed with the Book of Revelation." It is possible, however, for a religious body to affirm this in all sincerity while simultaneously denying either expressly or by implication that the Scriptures are sufficient. This feature is present in the position of the Roman Church; this denomination, though willing enough to admit that the canon is complete, subjects the Scriptures to its own authoritative interpretation, and places a body of tradition alongside them as the rule of faith and life.

Now when we come to the matter of the Adventist view of the work, especially of the writings, of Ellen White, we are confronted with a position comparable in some respects to that of Rome. For in *Questions on Doctrine* the denomination confesses:

> The Holy Spirit opened to her [Mrs. White's] mind important events and called her to give certain instructions

for these last days. And inasmuch as these instructions, in our understanding, are in harmony with the Word of God, which Word alone is able to make us wise unto salvation, we as a denomination accept them as inspired counsels from the Lord.[20]

At a later point we shall give some attention to what this position implies with respect to the authority and function of Mrs. White's writings. The broad observation should be made here, however, that the claim of a reappearance of the "Spirit of prophecy," as the Adventists use the term, is demonstrably incompatible with a serious commitment to the sufficiency of Holy Scripture. There are, after all, only two options available here. The one is that God, in His Word, has left nothing unsaid that it is necessary for men to know either as to faith or life. The other is that either ecclesiastical authority or additional special revelation is necessary to the completion or to the correct interpretation of Holy Scripture. And there is every indication that Adventism, though maintaining that it believes in the inspiration and authority of Scripture, chooses the latter alternative.

Now it may well be that Seventh-day Adventism has no particular zeal for the idea of the sufficiency of Scripture as defined above. In any case, it is important that the statements which it issues regarding the canon not be interpreted to mean that it holds that special revelation, in the full sense of that term, ceased with the last book of the Bible. For whatever else Seventh-day Adventism claims for the writings of Ellen G. White, it certainly regards them as being in a class distinct from and superior to merely human expositions of the Word. They are thus in some sense "new revelations of the Spirit."

The question remains, however, as to whether or not the Adventist view is more self-consistent and more congenial to the Bible's own representation of the work of the Holy Spirit than is the historical Protestant position. Is it possible, after all, that Holy Scripture allows for and even demands a latter-day prophetic ministry of the type which this movement judges Mrs. White to have performed? Seventh-day Adventism offers several arguments to support the affirmative answer to this question, arguments which many, obviously, have adjudged to be of sufficient

20. *Questions on Doctrine*, p. 93.

weight to warrant acceptance. It is necessary, therefore, that we take account of the more salient of these:

(1) *The Historical Argument*

Seventh-day Adventism holds that the "Spirit of prophecy" was intended to be God's abiding gift to His church, a normal means for the instruction, guidance and warning of His people in all ages. That it did not so remain with the church was the entail of certain ecclesiastical sins and shortcomings, pre-eminently those of the formulating of creeds and subservience to the pope.

Now it is true enough that after the age of the Apostles the church suffered a sharp decline both on the doctrinal and organizational sides. The Christian who for the first time is exposed to the writings of even the earliest of the so-called "Apostolic Fathers," with their incipient sacerdotalism and their more than incipient legalism can scarcely fail to be astonished that things should have deteriorated so badly and so soon. The Seventh-day Adventists, of course, are not the first to have marked this, nor the first to have addressed themselves to the problem of the cause of such a distressing development. Nor, indeed, are they the only ones who have ever sought to make church history serve their particular opinions. Superficial treatments of these questions abound; thus the stifling of missionary zeal and the deterioration of the quality of Christian living have been accounted for by such things as the preoccupation of the church's leadership with theology, the decline of a certain view of the sacrament of baptism, or the failure of Christendom at large to have acquiesced in some preferred construction of the events which would attend the second coming of Christ.

For Seventh-day Adventism, however, all is attributable to developing church organization and the emergence of creeds;[21] these were responsible for driving out the "Spirit of prophecy." To deny the validity of such an inference is not to say, of course,

---

21. The Adventists, and all other groups who deprecate organizations and creeds, would do well to ponder the fact that every association which acknowledges any sort of teaching to be true, has requirements for membership, or carries on an evangelistic, educational or literary program, dispenses with neither "creed" nor "ecclesiastical organization." The churches of apostolic times were both creedal and organized. The important question therefore is not *whether* but *what kind* of creed, church government and church program.

that church history can teach us nothing; developments in the early days of Christianity have lessons of great value for later generations, lessons which they have perhaps been all too slow in learning. It is of surpassing importance, however, that the historical data not be misread; that special pleaders for every shade of belief who try to make history prove what they desire it should prove not be permitted to go unchallenged. And, in fact, when the Adventist contentions are exposed to a critical examination it becomes evident that they are ill-supported by either history or Scripture.

For one thing, Seventh-day Adventism seems to be under a considerable illusion concerning the actual circumstances of the Christian church of the first century. Paul's letters to Galatia and Corinth, the book of Hebrews, or Revelation 2 and 3 provide all the evidence necessary to show that the church in apostolic times was anything but unmixed purity and love. Second, and more important, is the fact that even if the churches in which the Apostles were known had been far purer than we have grounds for believing that they were, and those of a few generations later far more corrupt than even their worst critics represent them as having been, this would have had little to do with the "Spirit of prophecy" being granted to the former and withheld from the latter. The coming of prophets to either Israel or the New Testament church had its divinely appointed reasons in connection with redemptive history, and those reasons had nothing to do with the merits of the people to whom they appeared. On the contrary, Elijah the Tishbite was sent to Ahab at a time when the Northern Kingdom was in a condition which, by comparison, would have made second or third century Christendom seem in a high state of spiritual health. Nor, for that matter, is there much to be said for the thesis that at all times during the centuries after the "Spirit of prophecy" is alleged to have disappeared, the Christian church, until *circa* 1850, was less worthy of the ministry of a prophet than was the generation of vipers of the days of John the Baptist.

(2) *The Argument from Scripture Texts*

In addition to their appeal to the history of Christianity, the Adventists bring several Scripture passages to bear in support of the claim that the "Spirit of prophecy" should have been

expected to reappear in the church. It will be of help both for
the purpose of evaluating Adventism's teaching on the doctrine
of the Word of God and for that of better appreciating its
general method of using proof texts if we examine some of these:

Revelation 19:10. This verse contains a phrase which is
employed with quite some regularity in Adventist expositions
of the subject of the gift of prophecy. A representative interpretation of the text has been cited earlier in this volume. The
reader, however, should be permitted to examine for himself
the movement's own explanation of the passage; we therefore
quote the exegesis offered by *Questions on Doctrine*:

> That expression "the testimony of Jesus" is clearly de-
> fined by the angel in Revelation 19:10. He says to John:
> "the testimony of Jesus is the spirit of prophecy." . . .
> The Spirit of prophecy is intimately related to the gift of
> prophecy, the one being the Spirit that indites the prophecy,
> the other the evidence of the gift bestowed. . . . The gift
> is the manifestation of that which the Spirit of God bestows
> upon him whom, according to His own good purpose and
> plan, He selects as the one through whom such spiritual
> guidance is to come. Seventh-day Adventists believe that
> this gift was manifested in the life and ministry of Ellen
> G. White.[22]

A reader of Adventist literature who had any misgivings at
this point would probably not have to consult more than a few
of the available commentaries on the book of Revelation to
discover that this verse is not among the more obvious passages
in a book which is throughout fraught with problems of interpretation. The Adventist view of the general meaning of the
text, while it agrees in some aspects with the consensus of several
of the more able expositors, does not reflect a particularly pains-
taking effort to come to grips with its real import. Indeed, it
is difficult to avoid the impression that this passage was seized
upon as an afterthought, with a view to giving plausibility to a
position which the movement is hard pressed to defend. There
is no satisfactory treatment, for example, of the important
question of whether the expression "the testimony of Jesus"
means the work of Jesus in testifying or testimony borne to

22. *Questions on Doctrine,* pp. 95f.

Jesus. Be that as it may, let it be supposed that the Adventist construction of the passage is generally correct, and let us over-look the fact that a good case can be made for the view that the verse envisions the Christian witness generally as well as the testimony of the prophet in the more restricted sense. What, even on this basis, does the verse prove with respect to the question at issue? Is it not to assign to it more weight than it can fairly be called upon to bear to find here justification for the idea that the church in subsequent ages would continue to be the object of specific, extra-Biblical revelations? As it stands, the text does nothing more than connect the testimony borne by or to Jesus with the Holy Spirit, that selfsame Spirit who is the Author of the prophetic Word. The extent of this work of the third Person of the Trinity, either as to time or as to the individuals through whom He speaks, cannot be decided by the contents of this verse. It is, therefore, extremely precarious to appeal to it as proof of the inspiration of a latter-day prophet; such a meaning could not well occur to any reader who had not been disposed previously to find it.

1 *Corinthians* 1:5-7; 12:1-11; *Ephesians* 4:11, 12. These verses are cited by Seventh-day Adventism to show that certain super-natural gifts were never intended to be only a temporary phenomenon but to be the abiding possession of the true church. The first passage, which comprises part of a thanksgiving uttered by the apostle Paul, praises God that "in every way you [the Corinthian Christians] were enriched in him with all speech and knowledge — even as the testimony of Christ was confirmed among you — so that you are not lacking in any spiritual gift as you wait for the revealing of our Lord Jesus Christ." The particular phrase by which the Adventists support the view that a church, if it is to enjoy all the blessings which are offered to those who rightly believe and faithfully live, should possess the gift of prophecy in the narrower sense, is that which reads, "so that you are not lacking in any spiritual gift." *Questions on Doctrine* interprets this to mean that "the church that would be waiting for the coming of the Lord would 'come behind in no gift,' that they 'may be blameless in the day of our Lord Jesus Christ.' "[23] They also remark: "We know that some earnest Christians have the impression that these gifts ceased with the

23. *Questions on Doctrine*, p. 94.

apostolic church. But Adventists believe that the closing of the
Scripture canon did not terminate Heaven's communication with
men through the gifts of the Spirit. . . ."[24]

The second passage (1 Cor. 12:1-11) is specific in its definition
of the "spiritual gifts" (v. 1) in terms of miracles, prophecies,
tongues, etc. All of these seem to have been present in abun-
dance in the Corinthian church.

The third passage (Eph. 4:11-12) enumerates the gifts which
God had placed in the church — "he gave some apostles, and
some prophets, and some pastors and teachers. . . ." The verse
1 Corinthians 12:28 is parallel to this, but includes certain gifts
not in the purview of the Ephesians passage — as miracles, helps,
healings, governments, diversities of tongues.

It is worth observing at the outset that the Adventists have
much company among groups in the general Christian tradition
who claim to possess at least some of the "gifts and manifestations" today. The life of Rome's far-flung millions is lived in an
atmosphere charged with the supernatural, especially with the
charism of miracles. And at the other end of the ecclesiastical
scale there is the phenomenon of Pentecostalism, the denominations comprising which are among the fastest growing in the
United States, if not in the world, and whose particular emphases
are the gift of tongues and miraculous healings. The entire
question of the cessation of such gifts goes considerably beyond
the scope of this study, but two remarks may appropriately be
made with reference to the claims of Seventh-day Adventism.

First, the argument that the Bible does not intimate that the
gift of prophecy was of temporary duration does not have much
force unless the Adventists are prepared also to take the position
that apostleship, tongues, and miracles were likewise intended
to be a normal feature of church life for all time. For when
we read carefully the listings in the passages from the Epistles
which include prophecy as one of the gifts, we find that they
include apostleship, diversities of tongues and miracles as well.
Nor is a distinction made among them as to which, if any, were
to be only temporarily with the church. Now as far as the writer
can determine, the Adventists do not lay claim to these other
endowments. They have no continuing apostleship, nor do
they speak in tongues, whether in the form of ecstatic utterances

24. *Ibid.*, p. 95.

or in that of intelligible speech in languages previously unknown. Indeed, if the following passage is representative, the
Adventist position on miracles in general does not offer much
more room for their reappearing than does that of most Prot-
testant churches:

> Shall one seek a religion that makes healing and miracle
> working the mark of its genuineness? . . . .
> There are four reasons why it is wholly unsafe to make
> miracles a test of true religion.
> *First, the miracle worker himself may be false.* . . .
> *Second, there may be healing without salvation.* . . .
> *Third, there may be salvation without healing.* . . .
> *Fourth, God does not always work in the same manner.*[25]

Precisely so. But the Seventh-day Adventists are the last
group in Christendom that should admit it. For if "the church
that is waiting for the coming of the Lord" should "come behind in no gift," must it not be evident that there is something
seriously at fault in a church which has the gift of prophecy
but lacks apostleship, tongues and miracles? And is not at least
the practical acknowledgment that this is the case with them a
tacit admission that it is indeed possible — and necessary —
to differentiate between those spiritual gifts which were characteristic of apostolic times and those which were to abide with
the church of Christ throughout its history on earth?

Secondly, the Adventist position on the subject of what is im-
plied by the statement, "so that you are not lacking in any
spiritual gift," is open to serious criticism. The point is not at
all well taken that a church is in some measure coming short in
its spiritual endowments if it understands that the gifts which
were directly revelatory in character — tongues, prophecy,
miracles, etc. — were withdrawn when the word-revelation in
the canonical books of Scripture was completed. True enough,
a church without wrinkle, spot or blemish has not yet appeared
on the scene of history. The Adventists are correct in observing
that the people of God, corporately as well as individually have
made nothing more than a small beginning of the new obedience
which God requires of them. But the reason advanced by

25. Arthur E. Lickey, *God Speaks to Modern Man* (Washington, D.C.:
Review and Herald, 1952), pp. 460f. Italics his.

Seventh-day Adventism for this state of affairs is one whose soundness may be categorically denied. No church suffers impoverishment because it has the Word of God, but lacks the gifts and manifestations. The plight of Christendom may be more fittingly ascribed to its failure consistently to apply that Word to itself, whether in doctrine or in life.

Matthew 7:10; 24:24; 1 *John* 4:1. These and similar passages, in the view of Seventh-day Adventism, imply the appearance of a line of true prophets in the last days who would be distinguishable from false prophets who would arise in the church to deceive it. In Froom's words, "Jesus warned against *false* prophets. . . . Would he not have warned against *all* prophets . . . if there was to be no true prophecy (in the last days)?"[26] Clearly the writer feels that an affirmative answer is required to this inquiry and that it is to reject a valid inference from Scripture to deny that prophets of the order of Ellen G. White are envisioned. The matter, however, is not quite so simple. These passages lose none of their cogency if they are understood to warn against *false* prophets not because there would also be *true* prophets in the same historical context, but because falseness would be their outstanding characteristic. There is an interesting parallel to this in the prediction by the apostle Paul that the coming of the "lawless one" will be "after the working of Satan with all power and signs and lying wonders" (2 Thess. 2:9). On the basis of the kind of reasoning which Adventism indulges, the true people of God must at such a time answer "lying wonders" with a demonstration of wonders which are the real thing. Nor is this all. The warning against false prophets and the spirit of antichrist may well have a broad application to all who corrupt the truth, who "preach another gospel which is not another," as well as to those who claim to have received supernatural revelations. The Christian answer to this is not the claim of direct communications from heaven, but the implementation of the true prophetic ministry — that of proclaiming the truth of the Word of God both to deceiver and to deceived.

(3) *The Argument from the Authority and Function of the "Spirit of Prophecy" Writings*

Having examined the claims of Seventh-day Adventism with

26. Froom, *op. cit.,* p. 970.

respect to the reappearance of the prophetic gift as such, we consider now the specific character of the writings of Ellen G. White. It is here that we shall attempt to decide the place which the "Spirit of prophecy" deliverances have in the denomination, and to show that the claims which Adventism makes for them are, on its own principles, self-contradictory.

THE AUTHORITY OF MRS. WHITE'S WRITINGS

We take account here of the appeal which Adventism makes to the class of prophetic utterances or writings to which they claim that the messages of Mrs. White belong. These, it will be remembered, are those prophecies, delivered either by speech or in writing during Biblical times, which did not find their way into the canon of Holy Scriptures.

At this point the Adventist position may be charged with a serious misunderstanding of the real character of the material which it finds analogous to the messages of Mrs. White. For it is to do an extreme injustice to the unrecorded prophecies which were given in the days when the Scriptures were still in the process of being completed to find in them the equivalent of writings which are not regarded "in the same sense as Holy Scripture" and which are "not to be equated with Scripture."[27] The fact is that the utterances of such people as Agabus or the daughters of Philip, or the written messages of Iddo the Seer, came to those to whom they were addressed with precisely the same authority as the canonical Scriptures come to the church today. Now we have seen earlier that Mrs. White looked upon her messages as being fully authoritative for those to whom she delivered them: "It is God," said she, "and not an erring mortal who has spoken." But if this be so, how can the Seventh-day Adventist Church press the distinction which it makes between these and the writings which were included in canonical Scripture? To the hearer of non-inscripturated prophecies as well as to the reader of the Biblical books applied the instruction and the sanctions given by the Lord through Moses in the words:

> I will raise them up a prophet from among their brethren, like unto thee, and will put my words in his

27. *Questions on Doctrine*, pp. 89, 93.

> mouth; and he shall speak unto them all that I shall command him. And it shall come to pass that whosoever will not hearken unto my words which he shall speak in my name, I will require it of him (Deut. 18:18-19).

The fact that many prophecies were of only temporary or local relevance had nothing to do either with their authenticity as communications from God, their authority, or their normative character. When God spoke to men through the prophets, those who were addressed had the Word of the Lord, and it was not for them to discern varying degrees of eminence in the words which they read or heard. For this reason it is difficult to understand why the Seventh-day Adventist denomination protests so vehemently against the charge that it regards the writings of Mrs. White as additions to the Scriptures or as messages to be equated with Scripture. If they are what they are claimed to be, they bear all the authority of the Word of God. And if the Adventists really believe that "the gift of the Spirit is one of the identifying marks of the remnant church"; that "this gift was manifested in the life and ministry of Ellen G. White";[28] and that "in ancient times God spoke to men by the mouth of prophets and apostles; in these days He speaks to them by the testimonies of His Spirit;"[29] why should they be reluctant to have them classified where they obviously belong — with the Scriptures of the Old and New Testaments? It may be, of course, that by "equation" with the Bible the Adventists have in mind some secondary features — whether the "Spirit of prophecy" writings should be called "Scripture," or the like. But there seems to be little room for doubt that with respect to the question of authority, the visions, writings, and whatever else is involved in the "gift," the utterances of Mrs. White are, for Adventism, on a par with canonical Scripture. What else is it possible to conclude regarding works of which it was said, "If you lessen the confidence of God's people in the Testimonies, . . . you are rebelling as certainly against God as did Korah, Dathan and Abiram."?[30]

THE FUNCTION OF MRS. WHITE'S WRITINGS

What does Seventh-day Adventism consider to be the purpose

28. *Ibid.*, p. 16.
29. White, *Testimonies*, IV, 189.
30. *Ibid.*, p. 362.

for which the "Spirit of prophecy" writings were given? Mrs.
White spoke of them as "a lesser light to lead men and women to
a greater light [the Bible]" and we have seen that Adventist
leaders refer to them as "an aid to a fuller, clearer understanding
of the Bible . . . a magnifying glass that brings out, not something
new, but details that might otherwise be missed by the unaided
human eye." Further, the Adventist doctrines were "simply
confirmed by the gift . . . or erroneous ideas pointed out." Does
the Adventist movement intend that the reader who is not of its
persuasion should be reassured by such statements? Are these,
after all, relatively modest claims?

Now there is a sense in which the analogy of a magnifying
glass can be applied to the ordinary preaching of the Word, or
to an honest commentary on some passage of Scripture. But
the sense in which this comparison is made, and the context
in which it appears, indicates an estimate of the writings of
Mrs. White more deferential than that which the Roman Church
scarcely accords to the words of the pope, who also "confirms
doctrines and points out erroneous ideas." Indeed, it might be
said of the writing prophets themselves that they were occupied
largely in bringing out details of the Law which otherwise
might have been missed. And when we remember that Mrs.
White, while at a meeting of the early Sabbatarian Adventists,
was able by prophetic insight to bid contending leaders in the
group to "yield their errors," it is difficult to avoid the conclusion that this "gift" had tremendously wide application.
And even if, for the sake of argument, it should be granted that
"Mrs. White's counsels do not bring out anything new,"[31] it is

31. There are, in fact, large blocks of material in Mrs. White's writings
which are extra-Biblical in every sense. For example, writing on the
subject of the boyhood of Jesus she says: "Because He was so gentle
and unobstrusive, the scribes and elders supposed that He would be
easily influenced by their teachings. They urged Him to receive the
maxims and traditions that had been handed down from the ancient
rabbis, but He asked for their authority in Holy Writ. . . . Jesus seemed
to know the Scriptures from beginning to end, and He presented them
in their true import. The rabbis were ashamed to be instructed by a
child. . . . They were angry because He did not obey their dictates.
Failing to convince Him they sought Joseph and Mary, and set before
them His course of noncompliance." — Ellen G. White, *The Desire of
Ages* (Washington, D. C.: Review and Herald, reprinted 1940), pp.
85-86. All this, of course, is highly inferential and probably wrong.
See Luke 2:52.

evident that this is in itself no mean gift. It does for the Adventists nothing less than to assure them that their distinctive views are indeed the sense of Scripture: that, for example, there is no room whatever for questioning the correctness of the "day-year" theory in the interpretation of Daniel 9:14, or the "continuous-historical" view of the book of Revelation, positions which, needless to say, would be regarded by many serious expositors of Scripture as doubtful in the extreme.

If the occurrences at Volney, New York, mentioned above, were at all typical, the "Spirit of prophecy," in that it revealed the one correct view of a given subject of inquiry, was used to cut many a Gordian knot in Biblical studies. By means of such an endowment the science of exegesis, if not rendered superfluous, would become much less complex. Thus the Adventists may say that their doctrines were "simply" confirmed by the gift of prophecy; but if this statement is examined more closely it becomes clear that the "magnifying glass" is very evidently more than the mere term would indicate; in an important respect this "magnifying glass" is reminiscent of Joseph Smith's magic spectacles, the "Urim and Thummin."

A further word should be said concerning the denomination's insistence that Mrs. White's writings are particularly for the Seventh-day Adventist denomination and not of universal application. It may be granted, of course, that certain prophetic deliverances in Biblical times were limited in their application to the individuals or groups to whom they were given. The words of some of the seers whose works are mentioned in the Old Testament, or of those who received the prophetic gift in New Testament times, were assuredly in such a class. But can the position be taken in all seriousness that writings which have been reproduced in multiplied thousands of copies, translated into dozens of languages, and distributed far beyond the confines of the Adventist constituency fall into such a category? Is it not something approaching a quibble to hold that a teaching is "present truth," to be preached in all the world, and at the same time to regard the writings in which this distinctive message is expounded as restricted in the scope of their application?

CONCLUDING SUMMARY

The foregoing analysis of the doctrinal statements of the Seventh-day Adventist denomination and of expositions published over the names of its standard writers leads to certain conclusions concerning their position on the subject of the Word of God:

(1) The affirmations of Seventh-day Adventism that the canon of Scripture is closed may be accepted only in a very limited sense; indeed, this sense is of such minor significance as to be all out of proportion to the movement's vigorous denials that it believes otherwise.

(2) The Adventist view of the restoration of the prophetic gift has only specious Scriptural support. The Biblical passages to which denominational writers appeal either prove more than the Adventists themselves admit, judging both by their silences and their positive practices, or they do not prove the point which they are attempting to make.

(3) The writings of Mrs. White, insofar as they are analogous to the prophetic ministry of the daughters of Philip, *et al.*, must, as far as their authority is concerned, be in a class with the books of the Bible.[32] The Adventists are inconsistent in denying that this is so.

---

32. The present writer has been unable to discover that Seventh-day Adventism makes any distinction among the various writings of Mrs. White; all seem to be "Spirit of prophecy" messages. The following from an official church publication is characteristic of its views on her works: "Here are two marvelous promises. . . . The first one is from St. Paul's writings. . . . The second one is from the writings of God's servant. She says: 'He who walks in the way of God's commandments is walking in company with Christ, and in His love the heart is at rest.' — *The Desire of Ages,* p. 331." Again, "On these . . . matters we need to be crystal clear as to what God requires. . . . We can know by diligently reading the Bible and the Spirit of prophecy." Theodore Carcich, "The Rewards of Obedience," *Review and Herald,* Jan. 16, 1958, pp. 3f.

CHAPTER THREE

SEVENTH-DAY ADVENTISM AND THE DOCTRINE OF MAN

THE MILLERITE MOVEMENT OF THE 1840's, FOR ALL ITS deviation from and polemic against the views of the second coming of Christ then current in Protestantism, tended to adhere to the historic doctrinal position of the several denominations on just about everything else. Thus William Miller lived and died a Calvinistic Baptist, and, has been noted earlier, many of the "Millerites," adjudging their prophetic convictions to have been in error, found no great difficulty in resuming their places in the life of those churches from which they had not, in general disassociated themselves.

The case was different, however, with those who in spite of everything still clung to the Adventist principles. Sabbatarian Adventism in particular began to take on a distinctive doctrinal complexion; as far as the doctrine of man was concerned, conditional immortality and annihilationism came to be characteristic elements of the message. It is not possible to say with certainty how it happened that such a departure from the confessional position of the churches early found wide acceptance in the Seventh-day Adventist ranks. However, since it is well known that some years previous to her becoming the vehicle of the "Spirit of prophecy" Mrs. White had found herself unable to accept the doctrine of eternal punishment as expressed in the creeds of Christendom,[1] one would not stretch the probabilities of the matter too far who ventured the suggestion that this was in large measure her own handiwork.

But Christianity is not a series of mutually isolated propositions; it is a system of truth in which no one can tamper with only a single part without affecting the whole. It was impossible, therefore, that Adventism could have merely let the idea of the eternal punishment of the wicked drop from sight and proceed as though nothing had happened. In order to remove

1. See Froom, *op. cit.*, pp. 978, 1033.

this particularly offensive element from its message, the denomination found it necessary to overhaul completely the fairly unanimous view of the Bible's teaching about human origins and the human constitution to which the Protestant churches adhered.[2] Joining Seventh-day Adventism in beginning at the beginning, then, we proceed to analyze its teaching on this subject.[3]

BODY AND SOUL

"Man was not in any sense created immortal. . . . Man was not in possession of an ethereal soul, or spirit, which survived death as a conscious entity apart from the body."[4]

It is in such fashion that the Seventh-day Adventists begin the positive exposition of their doctrine of man. In support of such a view of human nature they turn first to consider the Scriptural terminology for "soul" and "spirit." With respect to the word "soul" we are informed that we must derive the definition of the Hebrew word (*nephesh*) so translated from the account in Genesis 2 of the creation of Adam. The key to the Biblical doctrine of man is the text: "And the Lord God formed man of the dust of the ground, and breathed into his nostrils the breath of life, and man became a living soul [lit., 'soul of life']." This indicates for Adventism that the term "soul" denotes the animated body, not an incorporeal entity capable of separate existence. A further consideration which lends sup-

2. It is recognized, of course, that neither conditional immortality nor annihilationism are Adventist innovations. Such views have been held from time to time by various individuals from the early Christian centuries downward. As far as the writer knows, however, no church, and no group of any significance within any church, had ever included these doctrines in its official teaching until they appeared in "post-Disappointment" Adventist thought (the Advent Christian Church is at one with Seventh-day Adventism on this point). The literature on the subject is extensive, and it is not the intent of the present chapter to repeat what has been said, and said well, in the several systematic theologies and monographs. We are concerned here only to assess the line of reasoning and the exegetical methods by which Adventism expounds and defends its distinctive views.

3. *Questions on Doctrine* is the work of choice in which to find Seventh-day Adventism's fullest presentation of its position on this head of doctrine. Here the denominational writers answer queries regarding the immortality of the soul, the condition of man in death, and the punishment of the wicked. They have also collected quotations, amounting to forty-two pages, from various "Champions of Conditional Immortality."

4. *Questions on Doctrine*, p. 511.

port to this construction of the matter is that Genesis 1:20 (lit., "Let the waters swarm swarms of souls of life," or "individuals of life") speaks of the fish, and thus of all animals, as "souls." Hence it is more accurate to say that a person *is* a soul than to say that he *has a* soul. As to the Old Testament in general, *nephesh* can be and frequently is translated by the term "life"; on numerous occasions "person," "individual," or the appropriate pronoun would be the best rendering. In the New Testament, "soul" is translated from the Greek word *psuche* with the meanings of "life," "breath," or "soul." All of this warrants the conclusion that for the Biblical writers the "soul" does not represent an incorporeal part of man, but the whole man. "The soul cannot exist apart from the body, for man is a unit."[5]

The denominational writers deal with the word "spirit" in much the same manner. *Ruach* and *pneuma* in Old and New Testaments respectively do not mean by definition that there is in man "a separate entity capable of conscious existence apart from the body." Thus neither "soul" nor "spirit" are immortal; the text "God alone hath immortality" (1 Tim. 6:13-16) is held to teach that innate immortality is an exclusively divine quality. In fact, in 1 Corinthians 15:55 immortality is promised to the faithful at the second coming of Christ. It follows, therefore, that man does not possess immortality; he would not be urged to seek for it if he did (Rom. 2:7). A further point is that at the creation of man God threatened Adam with death if he disobeyed; hence he must not have been created incapable of dying.

Such is Adventism's position on man's nature. But if there is no separate, incorporeal entity in man, what, precisely, is the Bible's teaching as to the state of man after death? On this subject the writers of *Questions on Doctrine* offer a list of Scripture texts consisting largely of verses of the class of Ecclesiastes 9:5-6 and Psalm 146:3. 1 Corinthians 15:17-18 is also mentioned: "If Christ be not risen your faith is vain . . . then they that are fallen asleep in Christ are perished." The Adventists argue from these data that the Bible pictures death as involving the cessation of consciousness, and that the resurrection is the hope of the Christian; his expectation is always

5. *Questions on Doctrine,* p. 515.

directed to the reanimation of the body, and at the second coming of Christ he shall receive his reward.   The silence of those who in the Biblical record returned from the grave is explored in its bearing upon the question of whether the soul remains alive and conscious when the body is dissolved, as is the fact that "the divine Word definitely declares that 'David never went up to heaven!' (Acts 2:34)."

But anyone reasonably familiar with the contents of the Bible would begin to recall passages which seem to teach that there is a conscious state after death.   Hence the Adventists continue this section with an exposition of two of these, namely Philippians 1:23 and 2 Corinthians 5:8.   In connection with the former of these texts (". . . to depart, and be with Christ, which is far better") the question is urged:

> Why should we conclude from this remark that the Apostle expects immediately upon death to go at once into the presence of Christ?   The Bible does not say so. . . . Such is not a necessary implication . . . of the text.   In this particular passage Paul does not tell us when he will be with his Lord.   It should be observed that Paul does not tell us that it is his soul or his spirit that will depart. . . . When the time of leaving comes he departs, and the whole person goes.[6]

In the case of the latter passage ("We are confident, I say, and willing rather to be absent from the body and to be present with the Lord"), Adventism expends some effort to prove that this text does not support the notion that the believer is conscious in death; it does not teach that the being "present with the Lord" will follow immediately the being "absent from the body."   That there is the interval of death between the two experiences is found by the Adventists to be "just as logical as to believe that one immediately follows the other, and more so in the light of what the same Apostle has taught concerning the resurrection at the second coming of our Lord."[7]

The section on conditional immortality is brought to a conclusion with "An Appropriate Word of Caution," the burden of which is that it was none other than Satan who introduced

6. *Ibid.*, p. 527.
7. *Ibid.*, p. 529.

the idea that the sinner would live forever. This, of course, is derived from the words recorded in Genesis 3:4 in which the serpent says to Eve, "Ye shall not surely die."

So much for Adventism's view of the constitution of man. As we now attempt an evaluation of the distinctive teaching which comes to expression here, it is necessary first of all to offer some criticism of the method by which it is formulated. For *Questions on Doctrine,* as well as other works of this type which the movement has produced, gives the impression that an assumption which underlies its whole approach is that such issues can be decided by doing little more than fixing upon the etymology of certain terms and tabulating the instances of their occurrence in Scripture. Thus since *nephesh* as it is used in Genesis 2:7 refers to the whole man as a "living soul," and since "souls of life" is predicated of even the lower animals, the word must be understood in virtually every other text in which it appears to refer to an integrated unit of life or some closely related concept. This, therefore, excludes the possibility of a conscious entity which can survive the death of the body. Here, to be sure, Seventh-day Adventism has some notable company, for contemporary writers in the field of Biblical theology who are at one with this movement on practically no other point employ similar methods and reach similar conclusions, at least so far as the "Hebrew" conception of man is concerned. D. R. G. Owen, for example, says:

> The Hebrews, though ignorant of the actual physiological nervous system and brain, nevertheless in their own way recognized the dependence of psychical activity on the physical organism. . . . The Old Testament shares with modern science the idea . . . [of] the interrelatedness *and inseparability* of the "body" and the "soul."[8]

But although such a construction is plausible enough, especially when the Old Testament is taken by itself, it falls short of doing full justice to the Scriptural data as a whole. To be sure, there is nothing more basic to meaningful doctrinal inquiry than the study of the words employed in the Biblical texts; to dispense with the use of the dictionary would be a fatal misstep.

8. D. R. G. Owen, *Body and Soul* (Philadelphia: The Westminster Press, 1956), p. 176. (Italics added).

It must be insisted, however, that the task is not so easily finished. When all of the words of all of the texts which bear upon the subject have been defined, there remains yet much to be done. Systematic theology must also have its rights, meaning that Scripture must be compared with Scripture. The many-sided and complex subject of the Bible's doctrine of man has therefore not been exhausted when it is shown that *nephesh* and *psuche* are used throughout its pages in the sense of "life," "person," or "consciousness," and that *ruach* and *pneuma* are employed to describe the animating principle, with nothing in the terms themselves which may be taken to mean an ethereal entity which survives death. That is all true enough. But it does not mark the end of the debate, for the discovery of the meaning of the terminology is only the first step in answering the question of the view of man's constitution which, if not described in so many words in Scripture, is nevertheless presupposed in the numerous affirmations which it makes concerning him, and which underlies even incidental references to his origin, nature and destiny. Some investigation of the question of whether the contention that the soul cannot exist apart from the body represents faithfully the sum of the Biblical evidence is therefore appropriate. Several observations follow which will show that something can be said on the other side of the issue:

(1) In the first place, Seventh-day Adventism has erred in its construction of what is actually the historic Protestant position with respect to man's nature; in at least one area it has joined debate against a position which its opponents too would repudiate. That is to say, the best writers of the evangelical Protestant school have never hesitated to affirm that the Bible represents man as a unit. H. Wheeler Robinson (with whose formulation of this point the Adventists express their concurrence), in asserting that "the Hebrew idea of personality is that of an animated body, not (like the Greek) of an incarnated soul,"[9] would find support on this specific detail from as orthodox a writer as John Laidlaw, who says that it is "characteristic of the Old Testament Scriptures to assert the *solidarite* of man's constitution — that human individuality is of one piece. . . . This assertion is essential to the theology of the whole Bible." Again,

9. H. Wheeler Robinson, *The Christian Doctrine of Man* (Edinburgh: T. & T. Clark, 1947), p. 27.

Laidlaw says, "Man's one, though complex nature, is to be his nature forever."[10]

We may not, of course, deny categorically that the Christian church has been unduly influenced by a view of the immortality of the soul derived from Greek philosophy. It is sadly true that popular Christianity has all too often been permitted to entertain ideas of an inherently sinful body, or to overlook the fact that the ultimate hope of the redeemed of God is not an incorporeal existence but resurrection. This, however, is if anything the fault of Christian education, for the Protestant position is not at all ambiguous on the point that the righteous, having passed from this life, "behold the face of God in light and glory, *waiting for the full redemption of their bodies*," and that the bodies of the just, by his Spirit [shall be raised] unto honour, and made conformable to [Christ's] own glorious body."[11]   In view of this and many similar formulations by standard writers, Protestantism cannot fairly be charged with having, after the style of Plato, affirmed the soul at the expense of the body.

(2) The common Protestant position, which recognizes that there is in man an internal and intensive unity of the material and the non-material, is not embarrassed when it is called upon to account for the pervasive use of *nephesh* and *psuche* in the Bible to describe the whole man.   Such a feature is adequately accounted for by a common linguistic phenomenon: the Biblical writers have merely used the term which they regarded as describing the center of the personality figuratively for the entire person.   The use of "soul" in this sense in many languages, including English, spoken by groups in whose culture a dichotomistic view of man's constitution is deeply rooted, affords a significant parallel here.   Expressions such as "There wasn't a soul there" do not owe their existence as idioms to Seventh-day Adventism.   Moreover, this very unity, which the Scriptures accent and the creeds elucidate, is a sufficient reason for the comparative scarcity of Biblical references to the non-material aspect of man in abstraction from the totality of his being.   On such occasions, however, as are appropriate for reflection upon

10. John Laidlaw, *The Bible Doctrine of Man* (Edinburgh: T. & T. Clark, 1905), pp. 56f.

11. *The Westminster Confession of Faith*, XXXII, 1, 3. Italics added.

the incorporeal element as such, it is made quite naturally and without compromising in any way the reality of the unity.

On the other hand, upon meeting such passages as refer to the "soul," "spirit," or "self" in contexts which seem to require that these be construed in distinction from the body, the Adventists are compelled to take positions which, being dictated by dire theological necessity, are unnatural and forced. Their inter-pretation of Philippians 1:23 is a case in point. As has been noted above, the Adventists do not allow this passage as a proof text for a state of consciousness after death and before the resurrection. They support this contention by observing (i) that Paul does not say *when* he will be with Christ and (ii) that he does not say that it is his soul or spirit that will depart but that *he* will depart — the whole person goes. The Adventist writers inform us as to the first point that the same Greek word is used here to express departure as that used in 2 Timothy 4:6. It is *analuo*, which has the force of "to be loosened like an anchor." Now this may be profound philology, but it is difficult to see what bearing it has on the point at issue. The trend of Paul's thought in Philippians 1:22-23, to a reader who had no distinctive view of human nature to defend, would seem to be that he is at a loss to know whether to prefer a continuing existence in the flesh, or to depart to be with Christ. The former would be for the benefit of the Philippian church, and of Christians generally; the latter would be better for himself. But if the Adventists are correct, Paul would have no problem. There would be no advantage to departing, for to do so would not insure his being with Christ one moment sooner than if he remained, and continued by word and by example to be a means of blessing to his brethren. The argument that it is he, not his soul or spirit, that departs is of little point — this is no Greek liberation from the prison house of the body, but a recognition that the "ego" even in death is not separated from Christ. Sure-ly the correct interpretation of this expression of uncertainty on Paul's part is that he anticipated, in the period between his death and the resurrection of the righteous, a place in the realm of the "spirits of just men made perfect" (Heb. 12:23 — what can this text mean on the Adventist view?) and conscious bliss in the presence of the Lord.

Having made these preliminary observations, we must come to grips with certain representative objections made by the Seventh-day Adventists to the Scriptural basis of the common Protestant doctrine. These may better be discussed as a whole than by joining issue at each verse, and for this purpose may be divided into several groups:

The appeal to verses referring to the condition of man in death

In the Old Testament, especially in the Psalms and Ecclesiastes, there are more than a few verses which speak of the silence of the dead, the perishing of the dead man's thoughts, and so forth. These passages prove to the satisfaction of the Adventists that there is no continuation of consciousness or of any kind of activity after the occurrence of death. An examination of such texts in their setting, however, may very well lead to a conclusion different from that reached by Adventism, namely, that at the least they allow, and in some cases fairly well require, the construction that they refer to the dead not in an absolute sense but in their relationship to living persons or earthly activities.

An examination of one of these, selected at random, evinces this fact. Psalm 146:4, cited on page 522 of *Questions on Doctrine,* reads: "His breath goeth forth, he returneth to earth; in that very day his thoughts perish." This verse, however, is found in the course of an exhortation by the Psalmist that men should trust in God and not "in princes, nor in the son of man in whom there is no help." Why is this counsel to be heeded? It is because all men are subject to death; even the mightiest of them expire and are buried out of the sight of their fellows; all their designs and plans, everything that has relevance to this present form of existence, are finished completely and finished forever. This is what the text intends to teach; there is no reflection one way or the other upon the state of the person after death. Indeed, if it should be insisted that this and similar verses must be applied to the destiny of the individual in a rigidly literal sense, and that the writers of such passages had in mind to say everything that is to be said concerning death, one who believed in no kind of immortality or resurrection at all would be perfectly justified in finding support for his view in these words. Understood as referring to anything more ultimate than the phenomenal aspects of death, they fit a view of man of the type which B. B. Warfield classifies as "Pure Mortalism"[12] better than they do the doctrine of conditional immortality. Does not Ecclesiastes 9:5 say ". . . the dead know not anything, neither have they any more a reward; for the memory of them is forgotten"? Where, by Seventh-day Adventist canons of inter-pretation, is there room for even a "conditional immortality" here?

The appeal to passages referring to "immortality" and "life"

The Adventists argue that since "God alone hath immortality" (1 Tim. 6:13-16), man does not have it innately; further, since "man is urged to seek for immortality (Rom. 2:7), he does not now possess it."[13]

The former of these verses, Paul's words to Timothy, are among the favorite texts by which Adventism proves that man is not immortal, and at first glance it would seem that this is all they need to make their case; the verse says in so many words that immortality cannot be predicated of anyone but God. The difficulty is, however, that if the "immortality" which is envisioned here is of a kind which can be partaken of by a creature at all, the movement has on its hands a text which proves far too much. How, if "God alone hath immortality," can man have "conditional immortality"? It should be obvious, therefore, that Paul is at this point using the word in a sense in which it cannot be applied to any creature. This "immortality" is an exclusively divine quality; no angel or glorified saint, not to mention the demons or lost men, will ever possess it as God possesses it. Indeed, it is unlikely that any group in the history of Christianity, other than an occasional isolated and short-lived mystical sect, has ever taught that man does or shall have immortality in this sense, namely, as an original, eternal or neces-sary quality. Certainly when traditional Protestantism affirms that men are naturally immortal, it does not mean that they are so in the same way as God is immortal; it is using the term "immortal-ity of the soul" with respect to men in general as the equivalent of "endless existence."

12. "Annihilationism" in *The New Schaff-Herzog Encyclopedia of Religious Knowledge* (New York: Funk and Wagnalls Company, 1908), I, 183ff. Reprinted in *Studies in Theology* (New York: Oxford University Press, 1932), pp. 447ff.

13. *Questions on Doctrine*, p. 517.

The latter of these passages, Romans 2:7, speaks of "immortality" in still another sense. That this is so is evident from the context, in which the words "glory," "honour," and "peace" (v. 10) are conjoined with the "immortality" for which men are urged to seek. All of these are in antithesis to "indignation and wrath and tribulation and anguish," the lot of the unrighteous. The force of "immortality" here, then, is not quantitative, in the sense of bare continuance of existence (in which sense all men are "immortal"), nor is it that of eternal and original immortality (in which sense only God is "immortal"); this "immortality" is of a qualitative kind, connoting incorruptibility, in which sense it is used of the redeemed people of God and of no others. The same principle may be applied to those passages which speak of "eternal life" as the "gift of God." This is not a "gift" of endless existence, but of perfect blessedness "in the full enjoying of God to all eternity."

The appeal to passages referring to "death"

The situation here is parallel to that which was noted in the preceding section. "Death" is used in Scripture in more senses than one, and "cease to exist" is by no means its most frequent meaning. This is manifestly the case even on the Adventists' own principles; if there is to be any future punishment at all (as the Adventists say there will be), "annihilation" cannot exhaust the meaning of "death" as the "wages of sin." The term, as will be apparent when the question of annihilationism comes under discussion, is used in a fuller and far more sober sense.

The appeal to the use of "sleep" to refer to death

The point is emphasized by the Adventists that "the Greek words for 'sleep' . . . refer in many instances to the sleep of death."[14] In this connection they cite the remark of W. E. Vine:

> This metaphorical use of the word sleep is appropriate because of the similarity in appearance between a sleeping body and a dead body.

It is difficult to determine what the writers of *Questions on Doctrine* had in view in calling attention to this fact. Vine's observation is quite correct, and it is the interpretation placed

14. *Ibid.,* p. 521.

upon this terminology by the great host of Christian writers. "Sleep" is indeed a natural euphemism for death, referring to the appearances of things, no reflection upon matters more ultimate being intended. As far as the non-material part of man is concerned, therefore, it is impossible to decide from this expression, taken by itself, whether or not there is consciousness after death. There is, in fact, but one place in Scripture where the term "fall asleep" is used in close conjunction with a reference to the departure of the non-material part of man, namely Acts 7:59-60. Here, in the account of the martyrdom of Stephen, the verses read:

> And they stoned Stephen, calling upon God, and saying, Lord Jesus, receive my spirit. And he kneeled down and cried with a loud voice, Lord, lay not this sin to their charge. And when he had said this, he fell asleep.

The point will probably not need to be elaborated that this connection gives scant support to the view that to "fall asleep," used of death, implies that Stephen did not enter consciously into the presence of his Saviour and Lord.

ANNIHILATIONISM

Having once decided to do away with eternal punishment, as that term has been historically understood,[15] the early Sabbatarian Adventists were compelled to choose between the doctrine of universal restorationism and that of the final annihilation of the wicked. Rejecting the former as devoid of Biblical support, they chose annihilationism, and this has been a point of major preoccupation with them ever since. As the denominational writers treat of this subject in *Questions on Doctrine*, they undertake first of all to dispose of the popular notion that punishment is now going on:

15. Seventh-day Adventists affirm that they believe in eternal punishment. They say: "Everlasting bliss for the righteous, and eternal punishment for the ungodly, are plainly taught in Scripture" (*Questions on Doctrine*, p. 533). They mean by this, however, that the punishment is eternal as to its *result*, not as to its *process*. "It is not an endless process of punishment, but an effectual punishment which will be final and forever" (see *ibid.*, p. 540).

> Neither evil angels or wicked men are *now* receiving final punishment for their transgressions. Such punishments are still future. . . . The devils asked Him [Jesus], "Art thou come hither to torment us *before* the time?" (Matthew 8:29). Evil angels are *reserved* unto judgment (2 Peter 2:4), or "unto the judgment of the great day" (Jude 6). Concerning the wicked we read that God reserves "the unjust unto the day of judgment to be punished" (2 Peter 2:9).[16]

On the positive side, the penalty which the wicked will pay for their transgressions and their rejection of Christ is to die, be cut off, perish, be burned up, be destroyed. Various passages from the Old and New Testaments which use these expressions are cited, and the force of the terms found therein are explored. We read:

> They will not only burn, Greek, *kaio* . . . but they shall be burned up, *katakaio*. . . . They shall not only be destroyed, *apollumi*, . . . but be utterly destroyed, *exoluthreo*. . . .[17]

More of the same type of appeal is made to the Biblical usage of various figures and similes which illustrate the fate of the wicked. Thus the comparison of the wicked to combustible materials and to the overthrow of Sodom and Gomorrah demonstrates that the ultimate fate of the ungodly is extinction:

> Jude['s] . . . unique expression . . . "the vengeance of eternal fire" (Jude 7) . . . could not mean fire that would be eternally burning, for the cities are not burning today. Rather this fire would be eternal in its *results*.[18]

It is further remarked that such expressions as "everlasting," "eternal," "forever," and "forever and ever" usually bear a manifestly limited force when used in Scripture. Five reasons for rejecting "eternal torment" conclude the chapter. These are, in summary:

(1) The wicked do not possess everlasting life, which is a gift of God.

16. *Ibid.,* p. 535.
17. *Ibid.,* pp. 535-537.
18. *Ibid.,* p. 538f.

(2) Eternal torment would contradict those Biblical passages which speak of a time when sin and suffering "shall be no more."

(3) It would "provide a plague spot in the universe of God throughout eternity" which God himself could not abolish.

(4) It would detract from the attribute of love in the character of God, and postulate "the concept of a wrath which is never appeased."

(5) Christ, in his atonement, " 'put away sin' (Heb. 9:26) first from the individual and ultimately from the universe."

A long chapter entitled "The Rich Man and Lazarus" follows, the purpose of which is to prove that the parable is an *argumentum ad hominem*. In the Adventist view not only does the story not reflect an event or class of events which occurred historically, but it was not even intended to give information concerning the destiny of the wicked. It was designed merely to teach a certain lesson, using as a vehicle for imparting the message the (erroneous) views of the Pharisees on the subject of the state of the dead. The discussion of the doctrine of man is then brought to a conclusion with the recital of a long list of "Champions of Conditional Immortality." These range from Martin Luther to Reinhold Niebuhr.

We begin our assessment of this point of Seventh-day Adventism's teaching with a notice of the appeal of *Questions on Doctrine to* 2 Peter 2:4 and Jude 6. These texts, it will be remembered, are offered in proof of the conviction that punishment "is yet future, not now going on." As the Adventists say, it is evident that these passages speak of a judgment upon fallen angels which will take place in connection with the events of the end of the age: these are "reserved unto judgment," or "unto the judgment of the great day." But is *all* punishment of the fallen angels to take place in the future? Is there no sense in which they are being punished now? The writers of this section, doubtless due to an oversight, failed, in giving us the answer to these questions, to include all the material on the subject which these texts afford. That they did so is most unfortunate, for the words which were omitted from their citation of the verses are not without some bearing on the point at issue. In the interest, therefore, of placing all of the facts before the reader, we quote the passages in their entirety:

> For if God spared not the angels that sinned, but cast them down to hell [Greek, *tartarus*], and delivered them into chains of darkness, to be reserved unto judgment; . . . — 2 Peter 2:4

Likewise:

> And the angels which kept not their first estate, but left their own habitation, he hath reserved in everlasting chains under darkness to the judgment of the great day. — Jude 6.

Perhaps future editions of *Questions on Doctrine* will take account of these omissions; certainly the verses as they stand do not support the thesis that the punishment of the demons is *entirely* future. This is not to say, of course, that there is no difference between the present and final states of the fallen angels; the Adventists' appeal to Matthew 8:29 in this connection is well taken. It appears that we are not to understand "deliverance into chains" absolutely, as though there were no sense in which the demons are not bound, or no way in which they can influence the affairs of the present world. Certainly we are confronted here with a question concerning which the Scriptures say very little; in the nature of the case it might have been impossible for them to have said anything more. Be that as it may, the Adventist position on this point is plainly untenable; the demons are even now suffering punishment of a preliminary sort, and will be judged and condemned finally at "the great day." Calvin makes a characteristically penetrating comment on this subject:

> But we are not to imagine a certain place in which the devils are shut up, for the Apostle simply intended to teach us how miserable their condition is, since the time they apostasized and lost their dignity. For wherever they go they drag with them their own chains, and remain involved in darkness. Their extreme punishment is in the meantime deferred until the great day comes.[19]

Many of the other arguments of the Adventists in support of annihilationism need not be discussed at length; several of

19. John Calvin, *Commentaries on the Catholic Epistles* (Grand Rapids: Wm. B. Eerdmans Publishing Co., 1948), *ad Jude* 6, p. 436.

them are based on appeals to texts of the class of those discussed previously when "conditional immortality" was under consideration. Expressions such as "the wicked shall be cut off" (Ps. 37:9); "They shall not be" (Ps. 37:10); they "shall perish" (Ps. 37:20) are easily construed, and in the light of the contexts are best construed, as referring to the eventual helpless estate of all those who are in opposition to God, and as having nothing in particular to do with individual eschatology. Again, there are certain verses with an unquestionable eschatological bearing which, speaking of the destinies of wicked men or fallen angels, employ such terms as "be destroyed," "perish," etc. These, however, are used pervasively by way of contrast to those modes of expression by which the highest reaches of Christian privilege and blessedness are described, namely, "eternal life," "salvation," "the kingdom of God," and the rest. In Salmond's words:

> When Paul contrasts eternal life . . . with the 'wrath and indignation, tribulation and anguish' which are for them that 'obey unrighteousness,' he gives us to understand with sufficient certainty what he means by the *perishing* of which he proceeds to speak.[20]

The crucial point of the whole argument is the discussion of the force of "everlasting," "eternal," (*aionios*), "forever," and "forever and ever." With respect to the word *aionios* as used, for example, in Matthew 25:46 of the punishment of the wicked, the Adventists observe that the punishment in question here and elsewhere (2 Thess. 1:9; Mark 3:29; Jude 7) is indeed "eternal."   ⊢

> The eternal life will continue throughout the ceaseless ages of eternity; and the punishment will also be eternal — not eternal duration of conscious suffering, however, but punishment that is complete and final. This death will be eternal. . . .[21]

As for "forever and ever" (*eis tous aionas ton aionon*), the point is made that both in the Greek of the New Testament and in the Hebrew equivalent in the Old (*olam*), there is a limitation imposed "according to the object to which it is applied." Thus,

---

20. S. D. F. Salmond, *The Christian Doctrine of Immortality* (Edinburgh: T. & T. Clark, 1897), p. 621.
21. *Questions on Doctrine*, p. 539.

"The Passover was to be observed *forever* (Exod. 12:17); the slave is to serve his master *forever* (Exod. 21:6), etc." This principle is then applied to the passages which describe the misery of the wicked. With reference to Revelation 14:11,

> The smoke ascended and the divine record is that it ascended "for ever"! . . . What we behold here is a picture of absolute, complete destruction. So shall it be in the day of executive judgment when the wicked are destroyed.[22]

We do well to join issue with Adventist teaching on the subject of eternal punishment at the text Matthew 25:46, a place in which, speaking of the last judgment, our Lord Jesus Christ uses this term and the expression "eternal life" in absolute antithesis; the one is the destiny of the wicked, the other of the righteous. Now Seventh-day Adventism says that "eternal punishment" should be construed here to refer to the result and not to the process of punishment. This, however, can be done only by treating several important exegetical details in unwarrantably casual style. For one thing, since no intimation of a shift of emphasis appears in the verse, the sense which would commend itself as that intended by the speaker of these words is that duration is in view alike in the reference to "eternal life" and in that to "eternal punishment." This is not to say that the alternative which the Adventists offer is not possible on strictly philological grounds: "eternal" can be and sometimes is used to express a result rather than a process, as in "eternal redemption" (Heb. 9:12). But when such is the case, the term with which is it associated makes the force of the adjective unmistakable. "Punishment" (*kolasis*) is not such a term. Here the word itself carries the distinct connotation of the conscious experiencing of retribution. If Matthew 25:46 was not intended so to be understood, some unambiguous indication of this would have been expected, and that all the more when a change in the force of the word "eternal" is required in order to render the meaning which is proposed. It is likewise to be remembered that the Jews of Jesus' day believed that punishment would be of eternal duration.[23] But if this doctrine were basically erroneous,

22. *Ibid.*, pp. 542f.

23. There is no need to support this observation with quotations, as the Adventists themselves, citing Josephus, affirm that this was the case (see *Questions on Doctrine*, p. 562).

and, indeed, the dangerous perversion of truth which the Adventists make it out to be, Jesus would scarcely have expressed himself in a manner calculated to reinforce it. This applies as well to the use of *olam* and *eis tous aionas ton aionon*. The terms can, indeed, be limited by the context, but, to cite only one example, such an expression as "the beast and the false prophet . . . shall be tormented day and night forever and ever" (Rev. 20:10) would be, to say the least, an unusual way for Holy Scripture to convey the idea, "They shall be annihilated."

THE RICH MAN AND LAZARUS

The twenty-three pages of argumentation in *Questions on Doctrine* devoted to Jesus' story of the rich man and Lazarus (Luke 16:19ff.) attest to the fact that annihilationism does not find it easy to reconcile this passage with its teachings. There is, to be sure, much in the course of Seventh-day Adventism's treatment of this passage to which we need not take exception; the Adventists would find many from schools of thought other than their own who understand it as a parable, and a parable it probably is. Even among those who would hold that the passage is substantially historical there are few who would take the position that every element of it is to be understood in a slavishly literal fashion. The Adventist contention that the dialogue was wholly imaginary may be too extreme, but there is nothing in particular at stake in granting this point. It may also be conceded, in Plummer's words, that "it is not the purpose of the parable to give information about the unseen world,"[24] if what is meant by this is that we do not have here an historical atlas of heaven and hell.

Nevertheless, when all this has been said, the fact must not be overlooked that even if the passage is taken as an *argumentum ad hominem*, there must be a point of contact with reality somewhere along the way. Jesus would never have employed a figure of speech in which he intended no correspondence whatever to that which he was seeking to affirm. Scripture is not so haphazard in its use of literary devices; even where the language is most evidently metaphorical it never leads us astray as to what is being elucidated. For example, it is improbable that

24. A. Plummer, *A Critical and Exegetical Commentary on the Gospel According to St. Luke* (New York: Charles Scribner's Sons, 1914), p. 393.

Revelation 21:21 intends that we should understand the twelve
gates of the "city foursquare" to be twelve literal pearls, or its
street to be, in the physical sense, pure gold. This is, no doubt,
imagery meant to convey to finite minds a picture of ineffable
✝ glory. But only the most irresponsible kind of exegesis would
demand that the reader of these words desist from the conclusion that there is such a substantial entity as heaven, or that it is
a place of consummate blessedness. Now in the case of our
Lord's parable of the rich man and Lazarus, in which the central
point, around which everything else in the story revolves, is
the contrasting fortunes of two men after their departure from
this life, an error of the most serious proportions would have
been given credit if, as a matter of fact, there were no such
thing as consciousness after the death of the body.

"CHAMPIONS OF CONDITIONAL IMMORTALITY"

The array of theologians of every point of view whom the
Adventists have found to be in agreement with at least some of
their tenets respecting the nature and destiny of man is impres-
sive indeed. However, as the writers of *Questions on Doctrine*
remark, "Truth is not, and never has been, established by human
majorities." We therefore make only one observation here,
namely, that this host of names needs nothing quite so badly as a
thorough critical sifting. Some of the writers quoted (as Luther
and Tyndale) did not hold to "conditional immortality" at all,
but only, at least at the time of the writing of the words quoted
from their works, to some view of the unconsciousness of the
dead before the resurrection. Others on this list seem to have
been arguing merely against the Greek notion of the immortality of the soul (as Bishop J. S. Perowne and Franz Delitzsch).
Yet other names are associated with theological ideas so far
✝ removed from historic Christian orthodoxy that it is difficult to
understand what prompted the writers to include them.

CONCLUSION

The distinctive positions adopted by Seventh-day Adventism
in its teaching concerning the nature of man, conditional immortality and the punishment of the wicked do not do justice
to the Biblical data in the totality of their bearing upon these
✝ subjects, and at certain points of crucial importance require that

passages be interpreted in a sense which they cannot, by the use of sound exegetical principles, have. Taking into account the reasons offered by the writers of *Questions on Doctrine* for their rejection of the traditional Christian position, particularly their rejection of the doctrine of eternal punishment, we conclude this discussion with a few summary remarks.

(1) The objection that since "eternal life" is the gift of God it is impossible that the wicked should possess it has in substance been refuted above; it is based on a misconstruction of the meaning of this term in distinction from "endless existence." In John 3:36, for instance, "everlasting life" is promised to those who believe on the Son of God; to those who do not believe the penalty that "they shall not see life" is threatened. This "not seeing of life," however, is not co-ordinated by the passage with "being annihilated"; it is co-ordinated rather with being subject to the abiding wrath of God.

(2) The objection that the idea of eternal torment would perpetuate sin, suffering and woe, in contradiction to Revelation 21:4, which envisions a time when these things shall be no more, proceeds from something less than a just interpretation of the use of these words in this verse. The context points in quite a different direction. It is the people of God who are the subject of the promise of tears wiped away and of endless felicity; the situation of those who believe not is described in fearful terms in yet several more places before the end of the book (Rev. 21:8, 27; 22:15, 18, 19).

For a similar reason there is no use to urge, as Adventism does, that Christ "put away sin first from the individual and ultimately from the universe." Hebrews 9:26 does not speak of a work of atonement which is cosmic in this sense; verse 28 clearly qualifies the "put away sin" of verse 26 with the words, "So Christ was once offered to bear the sins of many." Likewise, if the words of Ephesians 1:13, 14 — "the Spirit of promise, which is the earnest of our inheritance until the redemption of the purchased possession" — prove that "the full fruition of Christ's sacrificial, atoning work will be seen not only in a redeemed people but in a restored heaven and earth,"[25] it may be con-

25. *Questions on Doctrine,* p. 543.

cluded that it is possible for any verse to be called upon to prove anything.

(3) Arguments of the class of "[eternal torment] in our thinking would detract from the attribute of love as seen in the character of God" are indicative of where this entire deprecation of the idea of unending retribution has its source. What we have here, one suspects, is a preconceived notion of what God's nature requires Him to do dictating what we may believe that He in fact does. Seventh-day Adventism has here taken the easy road, down which others in the history of Christianity have preceded it, and it has attempted, doubtless for what has appeared to it to be the best of reasons, to soften the stern realities of which Scripture speaks.

Assuredly, there are aspects of this datum of revelation, as there are aspects of all the ultimate questions of God's providential rule, of sin, and of judgment, which transcend the ability of the human mind to fathom. Adventism is here doing only the natural thing as it implements its desire to justify the ways of God before finite and sinful intellects. Men are not, of themselves, disposed to say, "Behold, I am vile; what shall I answer thee? I will lay mine hand upon my mouth." They do not, as a matter of course, check the rising doubt and the rebel sigh by asking themselves, "Who art thou, O man, that repliest against God?"

But the Christian may do nothing less. We are committed by our very profession of faith in Him whose ways are not our ways, and whose thoughts are not our thoughts, not to demand that the sovereign God adapt His judgments to our notion of what the moral order should be, but in the face of the most vexing problem of revealed truth to say, "Even so, Father, for it seemed good in thy sight." It has not been given to us to determine how sinful is sin, or to fix the degree of punishment which is due those who are in a state of rebellion against God, who then are we to say that infinite love and eternal retribution are incompatible concepts?

Our calling is to receive in humility and adoration what God has chosen to tell us concerning Himself, and to confess gladly that it is He alone who is qualified to define the limits within which His attributes may come to expression. When, therefore, orthodox Protestantism affirms, "Every sin deserveth God's wrath and curse both in this life and in that which is to come,"[26] it does not do so because of lack of altruism, much less because it entertains ideas which are the legacy of a corrupt church's efforts further to enslave the superstitious. It is because, yielding to the authority of Holy Scripture, in which it believes God has spoken, it finds it impossible to affirm anything else.

26. *The Westminster Shorter Catechism,* Q. 84.

CHAPTER FOUR

SEVENTH-DAY ADVENTISM AND THE PERSON OF CHRIST

IN MOST RESPECTS THE SEVENTH-DAY ADVENTIST VIEW OF THE person of Christ follows the lines of ecumenical orthodoxy.[1] One aspect of the denomination's position on this head of doctrine, however, has occasioned much discussion. This has to do with certain statements which appear now and again in Adventist literature on the subject of the human nature of Christ. A classic example of this is a passage in a widely used book of readings which has been reprinted many times:

> In His humanity Christ partook of our sinful, fallen nature. If not, then He was not 'made like unto His brethren,' was not 'in all points tempted like as we are,' did not overcome as we have to overcome, and is not, therefore, the complete and perfect Saviour man needs and must have to be saved. The idea that Christ . . . inherited no tendencies to sin, and for this reason did not sin, removes Him from the realm of a fallen world, and from the very place where help is needed. On His human side, Christ inherited just what every child of Adam inherits — a sinful, fallen nature. And this was done to place mankind on vantage ground, and to demonstrate that in the same way every one who is 'born of the Spirit' may gain like victories over sin in his own sinful flesh.[2]

1. It should not be overlooked that there have been, and apparently are now, small minorities in the church whom *Questions on Doctrine* describes as "the few so-called Arians among us" (p. 48). These evidently hold to something less than the full doctrine of the deity of Christ. The toleration of such is explained by the Adventists on a pragmatic basis: Mrs. White is quoted as having said, in substance: "No matter how right you are, do not stir up the subject at the present time because it will cause disunity." Adventists ascribe these words to the "Spirit of prophecy." Others may discern in them a closer resemblance to the "spirit of the age."

2. *Bible Readings for the Home Circle* (Mountain View, California: The Pacific Press Association, 1916), p. 173.

There are other passages from representative Adventist writers which have also given reason for critics to charge that Adventist doctrine is seriously at fault in its view of the person of Christ. For example, L. A. Wilcox, writing in the denominational periodical *Signs of the Times,* said:

> In His veins was the incubus of a tainted heredity, like a caged lion, ever seeking to break forth and destroy. Temptation attacked Him where by heredity He was weakest — attacked Him in unexpected times and ways. In spite of bad blood and inherited meanness, He conquered.[3]

Words could scarcely state more plainly that, for Adventism, the incarnation of the Son of God involved not only His becoming flesh, but sinful flesh. Nor does what they say respecting the liability of Christ actually to sin dispel the suspicion that such is the case. The following from Ellen G. White is characteristic:

> Into the world where Satan claimed dominion God permitted His Son to come, a helpless babe, subject to the weakness of humanity. He permitted Him to meet life's peril in common with every human soul, to fight the battle as every child of humanity must fight it, at the risk of failure and eternal loss.[4]

More recently, William Henry Branson, one of Adventism's standard writers, observed:

> The Catholic doctrine of the "immaculate conception" which holds that Mary, the mother of our Lord, was born without the taint of sin, attempts to separate Christ from the common inheritance of the human race. From this springs

3. Quoted in L. T. Talbot, *What's Wrong with Seventh-day Adventism?* (p. 24), from *Signs of the Times,* March, 1927. The writer is aware that certain Adventist leaders consider this quotation unrepresentative. Other Adventist workers with whom he has discussed this matter, however, have not heard of its having been disqualified as denominational material, and have sought to defend it and similar formulations by an appeal to Romans 8:3. The denomination as a whole has apparently never repudiated it. The facts that the statement is baldly heretical by any Christian standard, and that Wilcox was a prominent Adventist leader combine to make such an action imperative if, indeed, this has no place in the movement's teaching. The writer will be happy to take cognizance of any further developments in the denomination's position in later printings of this work, if any.

4. White, *The Desire of Ages,* p. 49.

the teaching that Christ was not really tempted and could
not have sinned. This belief cuts off the lower rungs of the
ladder, and leaves men without a Saviour who can be
touched with the feeling of men's infirmities, and who can
sympathize with them in their temptations and sufferings.
By this teaching the essential humanity of Jesus is denied.
Thus the ladder does not reach to the earth where men are.[5]

The ordinary reader of such words would inevitably conclude
that Seventh-day Adventism intends to affirm that Christ possessed
a sinful human nature. But language can be deceptive, and
Seventh-day Adventism seems never to have made it a matter of
policy always to present its case so as to make misunderstanding
impossible. Its insistence that things are not what they seem
with its teaching at this point must therefore be reckoned with.
Questions on Doctrine offers something which, in view of its
writers, is a reasoned exoneration of the movement's theology
from any suggestion of heterodoxy. The argument may be
summarized as follows:

(1) The Son of God, in His incarnation, took humanity upon
Himself, becoming "one with the human race that He might
reveal the fatherhood of God to sinful man, and that He might
redeem lost mankind."[6] Though He became flesh, with all its
infirmities, He was never anything less than the blameless Son
of God. Though touched with the feeling of our infirmities,
He never sinned. He was the God-man, the second Adam, who
came "in the likeness of sinful flesh," but He Himself did not
have any of its sinful propensities or passions: He was without
the taint of sin. "We emphasize again," they write, "that in
His human nature Christ was perfect and sinless."[7]

(2) The Son of God, in counsel with the Father, took upon
Himself the burden and penalty of our sins. But this does not
mean that there was the slightest taint of sin upon Him; He did
not become a sinner. He, though guiltless, bore the punishment
of the guilty as their *substitute*.

(3) But the iniquities of sinful men is not all that Jesus
bore: there was something further that He took upon Himself.

5. W. H. Branson, *Drama of the Ages* (Washington, D. C.: Review and
Herald, rev. ed.), pp. 101ff.
6. *Questions on Doctrine*, p. 51.
7. *Ibid.*, p. 55.

What the Adventists have in mind here is suggested by Isaiah 53:3-4 and the comment upon this passage in Matthew 8:17. They say:

> As He bore (Gr. *phero*-LXX) our iniquities (Isa. 53:11) so He bore (Gr. *anaphero*) our weaknesses (Matt. 8:17, Weymouth).

> But let us observe further what is implied in this. Notice the words used to express the thought, both in Isaiah 53 and Matthew 8. He bore our *griefs*, our *sorrows*, our *infirmities*, our *sicknesses*. The original words are also translated *pains*, *diseases* and *weaknesses*.

The point which the Adventists are attempting to make is this:

> It could hardly be construed . . . from the record of either Isaiah or Matthew that Jesus was diseased, or that He experienced the frailties to which our human nature is heir. But He did *bear* all this. Could it not be that He bore this *vicariously* also, just as He bore the sins of the whole world?[8]

By way of further explication the Adventists say that weakness, frailties and failings are things which are natural to sinful men. Christ, however, took these not as something innately His; He bore them as our substitute. The writers of *Questions on Doctrine* plead that this is the sense in which occasional remarks in the writings of Mrs. White to the effect that Christ took "our sinful nature" should be understood. Considering that she speaks pervasively in her works of the sinlessness of the human nature of Jesus, when she says now and then that Christ took "man's nature in its fallen condition" she is to be understood as speaking of a *vicarious* bearing "of the burden and penalty of our iniquities, or the diseases and frailties of our human nature."[9]

This, then, is Seventh-day Adventism's exegesis of the "Spirit of prophecy" writings in those places where they treat or allude to the doctrine of the person of Christ. One might well wish that the subject could be dropped at this juncture; certainly if contemporary Adventist opinion wishes to express agreement with the general Protestant position on this detail, it would be nothing more than the charitable thing to desist from pressing

8. *Ibid.*, pp. 58-59.
9. *Ibid.*, pp. 61f.

the point that not only do the source materials provide ample
room for a less favorable interpretation, but that the very
explanation of these which Adventism offers contains elements
which are confusing and self-contradictory. But, unfortunately,
there remain questions about this issue which not even the most
sympathetic criticism can well refrain from raising, this not in the
interest of keeping alive a debate which would better be allowed to die, but in the hope of arriving at an understanding of
the real state of affairs.

First, then, we take account of the Adventist construction of
Christ's "vicarious" suffering. No evangelical, certainly, will
object to the view that the entire course of the humiliation of
the Son of God was for the sake of sinners. Every branch of
Christ's church would confess that His birth in a low condition
and His undergoing the miseries of this life, as well as His
dying on the cross, was in behalf of lost men. This involved
the Saviour's suffering many of the sinless infirmities to which
humankind is subject — weariness, hunger, pain and the rest.
It involved no less His being brought daily "in contact with the
thousand forms of want and woe, of discord in man's outer
life, of discord in man's inner being. Every one of these, as a real
consequence of sin, and at every moment contemplated by him
as such, pressed with a living pang into the holy soul of the
Lord."[10]   In all probability this is the sense in which Matthew's
Gospel speaks of Christ's taking our infirmities and bearing our
sicknessess.

Now the Adventists describe this as a "vicarious" bearing of
human weaknesses. To do so, it may be supposed, is possible
if the reader is careful to investigate what the authors had in
view in their use of this term. The choice of this word, however,
may be seen to be an unhappy one when it is considered that in
the history of Christian doctrine "vicarious" has come to be
used with special reference to the atonement of Christ for
sinners, and to convey the truth that He bore the full penalty
of their sins that they might not have to bear it. The situation
worsens, however, when this "vicarious" bearing of human
infirmities is described in terms of Christ's taking "our sinful

10. R. C. Trench, *Notes on the Miracles of Our Lord* (New York:
Fleming H. Revell Company, n.d.), p. 185.

nature."[11]   The use of language with such a precise theological meaning as the words "sinful nature" in such a strange sense would be censurable in the veriest novice; in writings alleged to be a "magnifying glass" designed to bring out the true sense of Scripture such a blunder is inexcusable.   Far from being "forceful, cogent statements,"[12] these words of Mrs. White tend to confusion at a point where perspicuity is not only possible but mandatory.

Exculpation on the grounds of carelessness in the use of terms, however, is not possible in the case of the passages cited from the other Adventist writings.   As a brief analysis of each of these three statements will demonstrate, the objectionable elements are too closely connected with the course of the argument for there to be any misunderstanding.

(1) In the passage from the denominationally edited *Bible Readings for the Home Circle*, the writer takes the position that in order to demonstrate that the renewed sinner can "gain like victories over sin in his own sinful flesh," Christ inherited all that men inherit — a sinful, fallen nature.   This, in his view, is required in order to exclude discontinuity between the probation of Christ and that of His brethren.   There can be no question that this is the force of what he intends to inculcate when he specifically repudiates the notion, unexceptionable to evangelical theology, that "Christ inherited no tendencies to sin and for that reason did not sin."   What can "tendencies to sin" mean other than the possession of the inclination, the bent, the disposition actually to transgress?

(2) The passage from L. A. Wilcox's article is, if anything, more explicit still.   The figure of a "caged lion ever seeking to break forth and destroy" is scarcely a similitude which gives rise to amiable associations.   Rather it conjures up in the mind the picture of a certain potential for violent excitement, a potential which is kept from becoming actual only by the imposition of external, unyielding restraints.   It is difficult, therefore, to imagine how any manipulation of the words could make such a simile translatable into something so innocuous as Christ's being subject to the pains and privations which all men have suffered since the fall, or even His "vicarious" bearing of

11. *Questions on Doctrine*, p. 60.
12. *Ibid.*

the evils which are the fruit of sin. Wilcox's statement cannot be reconciled with the Adventist confession that Christ came "in the likeness of sinful flesh," but without a taint of its sinful propensities and passions.

(3) William Henry Branson's work from which the third passage is quoted was copyrighted in 1950, meaning that official Adventism had had several decades, at least, in which to ponder the fact that it was being charged by conservative Christians with holding erroneous views of the human nature of Christ. Thus, if Branson and the denominational publishers had not wished to do anything in a positive way about correcting the unfortunate blunders of the earlier works, the least that they might have been expected to do was to avoid giving the impression that they concurred in them.

What they did in fact was to espouse, in language quite as specific, the same errors as the others. Thus in his discussion of the coming of Jesus to the world, Branson criticizes the Roman doctrine that Mary His mother, by virtue of her immaculate conception, was herself free from original sin. Now it is entirely appropriate for a writer expounding the doctrine of the incarnation of the Son of God from the standpoint of the Protestant tradition to repudiate this Scripturally indefensible fabrication. Branson, however, is at pains to make the point that the fallacy of the "immaculate conception" is that in preserving Mary from original sin it deprives the human race of a Jesus who partook of man's sinful nature, and gives us a Jesus who was unable to be touched with the feeling of man's infirmities. We need not discuss here the writer's mistaken notion that the Romish position implies that Christ was not truly human. We observe, however, that this passage affirms in unmistakable language that a Mary who was free from original sin could not have communicated a sinful nature to her Son. Moreover, there is no attempt made to guard against the impression that it is, indeed, original sin which is here being ascribed to Jesus.

CONCLUSION

Questions on Doctrine goes to some lengths to demonstrate that Seventh-day Adventism affirms the sinlessness of the human nature of Christ. It is to be hoped, certainly, that the real Adventist position on the subject is reflected here; it is also to be hoped that those who define the doctrines of the movement will be led to abandon such unhelpful terminology as Christ's "vicarious" taking of a sinful human nature. But what of those passages in the church's literature, not mentioned either in the text or the fourteen-page appendix of quotations from Mrs. White and other representatives of the movement on this subject, which distinctly teach that Christ had a sinful, fallen human nature? It is hardly possible that the denomination does not realize that these exist; its critics have cited them time and again.[13] Nor is the plea well taken that these writers are a "fringe group" or that such statements "crept in." The authors from whose pens this material has come are among the church's prominent apologists, and the works in which it appears were published by the denominational press. The only conclusion possible is that we have here an apparent contradiction in Seventh-day Adventism's teaching, a contradiction of a most serious kind, for what is involved is nothing less than the integrity of the person of Jesus Christ. If, therefore, it is expected that those who are aware of the position which some of the church's writers have taken on this subject shall accept its protestations of Christological orthodoxy, an airing of these materials and a repudiation of the ideas which they propagate ought to be forthcoming.

13. As J. K. Van Baalen in *The Chaos of Cults;* L. T. Talbot in *What's Wrong with Seventh-day Adventism?* among others.

CHAPTER FIVE

SEVENTH-DAY ADVENTISM AND SALVATION

IN THE SURVEY OF SEVENTH-DAY ADVENTISM'S BEGINNINGS GIVEN in the first chapter of this study, it was shown that Hiram Edson's vision on the morning after the "Great Disappointment" of October 22, 1844 was soon accepted by a number of the Millerite groups as the solution to the problem of the failure of the Second Advent to come to pass as expected. This position, the validity of which was confirmed by the prophetic insight of Ellen G. White not many months after it was formulated, became one of the "foundational doctrines" of Seventh-day Adventism, and has remained ever since an extremely important aspect of its teaching.

It could not have been otherwise than that this new development should have had far-reaching effects upon Adventist doctrine as a whole. The thing asserted demanded the working out of its implications, and the doctrine of salvation, of course, was the area of theology most profoundly affected. It is not to take liberties with the historical facts to observe that the whole question of the meaning of the atonement and heavenly intercession of Christ was oriented to the new teaching; in other words, Edson's vision of the heavenly sanctuary became the axiom from which Adventism's distinctive estimate of the work of Christ was derived.[1]

---

1. Froom clearly indicates that this was, in general, the course of the development of the doctrine as he writes: "From Edson's dawning concept of Christ in the most holy place, now engaged in His special ministry there, he and his associates had been persuaded that a comprehensive study of the *typical* sanctuary service, on earth, must be made from the Scriptures in order to understand the antitypical sanctuary service in heaven and the character of that phase of ministry upon which Christ had just entered. So with Bibles and concordances they diligently pursued their way through this fascinating field of study. The sanctuary and its service, given through Moses to Israel of old, they found was instituted to portray annually certain visible, understandable lessons compassing the entire plan of salvation" (Froom, *op. cit.*, pp. 895ff.).

THE HEAVENLY SANCTUARY

Inasmuch as the Adventist doctrine at this point had its genesis in a particular view of the high priestly ministry of Christ, its main emphasis, and its most marked deviation from the traditional Christian positions, are on the subject of the *nature* of the atonement.[2] Seventh-day Adventism's teaching, which is to be found in any presentation of its doctrine which is at all comprehensive, may be set forth as follows:

(1) The sanctuary built by the Israelites in the wilderness after the pattern which had been revealed to Moses at Mount Sinai was divided into two apartments in addition to the outer court. These were the holy place and the most holy place.

(2) Various sacrifices were offered in the outer court daily throughout the year, all of which pointed to Christ, who was to be sacrificed once for all for the sins of man. The morning and evening sacrifices spoke to the people of God's provision for their salvation:

> Wherever the Israelites lived they could turn toward Jerusalem at the time of the morning and evening sacrifices, confess their sins, and know that their God would graciously forgive.[3]

The other offerings, however, were brought by individual members of the congregation, and did not represent God's provision for salvation but the sinner's response to that provision. There was, therefore, a marked difference between the two classes of offerings. The "continual" was offered on behalf of the sinner whether he sought its benefits or not. The several individually provided offerings, however, were brought by the sinner, who acknowledged by laying his hands on the head of the animal before it was slain

2. On the question of the *necessity* of the atonement, Seventh-day Adventism, although it does not use such terminology, appears to take the position described in the classical Protestant literature as that of "consequent absolute necessity." Branson is typical as he remarks: "There was . . . only one way to save doomed man from eternal death, and that was for God, as man, to become man's surety, assume his guilt and die in his stead. This He did not hesitate to do. He gave His only-begotten Son as a ransom for the fallen race" (*Drama of the Ages*, p. 110). As to the *extent* of the atonement, their view is that of evangelical Arminianism (see *Questions on Doctrine*, pp. 404ff.).

3. *Questions on Doctrine*, p. 359.

that it was his substitute. Thus the "continual" was *primary*, the others *secondary*.

> "The morning and evening sacrifice was fundamental, . . . the type of what was accomplished on Calvary's cross in antitype for all mankind."[4]

The Adventists see in these two groups of sacrificial offerings, then, the themes of "provision" and "acceptance." The "acceptance" is the Old Testament equivalent to conversion or the "new birth."

(3) In the daily sacrifices, some of the blood of certain offerings was brought into the holy place, and either sprinkled before the veil which separated the holy and most holy apartments, or placed upon the four horns of the altar of incense. By this means the sins of the people were borne symbolically into the sanctuary, to the entrance of the most holy, which was thereby "polluted."

(4) The service of the annual Day of Atonement, which took place on the tenth day of the seventh month, involved the "cleansing" of the sanctuary. On this day the high priest entered the most holy place with the blood of a sacrifice, which he sprinkled upon the mercy seat. After this he went outside, thus symbolically removing the sins of the people from the sanctuary. At this point the "atonement" had been accomplished. But the service, typical of Christ's work in behalf of sinners, was still incomplete, for once outside, the priest, by placing his hands on the head of the live "scapegoat," transferred in symbol the sins of the people to the animal, and sent him away into the wilderness to die. It was at this point that the work of the cleansing of the sanctuary was finished.[5]

(5) The earthly sanctuary and service were, according to the book of Hebrews, a "copy and type of things heavenly." In the earthly tabernacle the *forgiveness* of sins was typified by the daily sacrifice and the taking of the blood of the lamb into the sanctuary. But the *blotting out* of sins did not take place until the annual Day of Atonement. To the question, "How does this have significance for the work of redemption accomplished by Christ?" the answer of Seventh-day Adventism is:

4. *Ibid.*, p. 360.
5. See Froom, *op. cit.*, p. 897.

The service in the first apartment symbolized the mediation of Christ for His people in all generations. And the final service, in the second apartment, on the Day of Atonement, symbolized the concluding judgment hour phase of Christ's ministry, preparatory to the final blotting out of sin. The sacrifice is the giving of the life of Christ Himself for the sins of men. And the scapegoat . . . symbolized Satan, the instigator of sin, who *after the atonement was finished* through the substitutionary sacrifice, bears his share of responsibility for all sins, and is banished at last into the abyss of oblivion.[6]

In summary, then, the Adventist view of the nature of the atonement of Christ is that, on the analogy of the ritual of the Old Testament sanctuary service, his death on the cross *provided* atonement. His high-priestly ministry, however, in which atonement was and is *applied*, consists of two phases. The first of these took place in the holy place of the heavenly sanctuary. From the beginning of His ministry in heaven until the year 1844[7]

6. *Ibid.*, pp. 898f.

7. According to the Adventist interpretation of the prophetic Scriptures, "God . . . fixed a definite time for the beginning of the final judgment. The time is not a secret. It has been revealed to His people, even to the very day" (*Drama of the Ages,* p. 327). This day, of course, was October 22, 1844, as attested not only by Daniel's vision of the 2300 days, but also by the clear teaching of the angel Gabriel in Dan. 9:24-27, in connection with the vision of the seventy weeks. Branson regards this latter passage as affording the material by which the reader may "compute a number of most important and astonishing prophetic dates" (*ibid.,* p. 331). These dates include the precise years of the rebuilding of Jerusalem (408 B.C.), the baptism of Jesus (A.D. 27), the crucifixion (A.D. 31), and the martyrdom of Stephen (A.D. 34). All this makes inescapable the inference that the "cleansing of the sanctuary" indeed began in 1844 and that the "work of final judgment [has] actually been going on in heaven for more than a full century." And lest it be thought that these calculations are in the realm of things debatable, Branson adds: "No other conclusions can possibly be reached through a candid study of the . . . declaration of the angel Gabriel to the prophet Daniel" (*ibid.*).

There are a number of other exegetical questions, too complex for treatment here, involved in the Adventist view. They see, for example, the beginning of the investigative judgment predicted in a number of passages in both Old and New Testaments. These include the "placing of thrones" in Dan. 7:9-10; the coming of the Son of Man to the Ancient of Days in 7:13; the prophecy in Mal. 3:1-3 of the coming of the Messenger of the Covenant to purify the sons of Levi; the opening of

He was making intercession for repentant sinners, offering up their prayers to the Father, and pleading His shed blood as the ground of their pardon. But the sins which they confessed were not "blotted out"; they were, rather, "transferred" from themselves to Him. Thus during all this time the sins of the saints were being placed on record in the sanctuary.[8] In 1844, however, Jesus the great high priest passed into the most holy place in the heavenly sanctuary, there to begin the solemn work of cleansing it from the sins which had, over the years, been accumulating there. This ministry was typified by the Day of Atonement service under the Mosaic law. The question arises at this point as to the precise character of the work of Christ in the most holy place. It is here that the concept of the "investigative judgment" appears, and here the discussion of the Adventist view of the doctrine of salvation moves to the subjective side, that is, to matters involving what is done in and for the believing sinner as a result of Christ's redemptive work:

THE INVESTIGATIVE JUDGMENT

The Adventist teaching with respect to the nature and purpose of this judgment is summarized as follows in a passage from the writings of Mrs. White:

> Attended by heavenly angels, our great High Priest enters the holy of holies and there appears in the presence of God, to engage in the last acts of his ministration in behalf of man, — to perform the work of investigative judgment, and to make an atonement for all who are shown to be entitled to its benefits.[9]

It cannot be too strongly emphasized that this judgment concerns only those who are believers in Jesus Christ, for the judgment of the wicked is not in view here. That this is the case

---

the books in Rev. 20:12-13, and others. In general, the Adventists take passages commonly regarded as referring to the Messianic age comprehensively, or to the eschatological consummation, as descriptive of the beginning of the "investigative judgment," culminating in the return of Christ in glory.

8. Branson, *Drama of the Ages,* p. 289.

9. E. G. White, *The Great Controversy Between Christ and Satan* (Washington, D. C.: Review and Herald, reprinted 1950), p. 475.

readily appears from the character of the typical service. Here only those Israelites who had confessed their sins and repented of them had their sins transferred to the sanctuary, from whence they were removed on the Day of Atonement. So it is that in the investigative judgment in the heavenly sanctuary the only cases which appear are those of professed believers. *"Confessed sins* alone," says Branson, "are placed under the sacrificial blood."[10]

What, then, for Adventism, is the meaning of the forgiveness of sins and the acceptance of the sinner as righteous in God's sight? Branson, dealing with the question of whether sins, confessed and forgiven are removed from the sinner, replies:

> [They are], so far as the individual is concerned. But this does not mean that the sins are at the time finally disposed of. Christ removes them from the records in the books of Heaven, but they are then charged against Him. He takes the responsibility for the sins and imputes His righteousness to the sinner. The record of sins still re- mains, only now they stand no longer charged to the one who committed them but to Christ his substitute. He has become the sin bearer, . . . but the record of sin, now transferred to the sanctuary, must remain until the judg- ment.[11]

During this investigative judgment, Christ is making a very careful examination of the records to see whether those who accepted Him are still worthy. Thus the judgment is for the purpose of ascertaining, before the final hour, who are en- titled to the benefits of Christ's atonement. The question of who these might be is a matter of crucial import, and the fol- lowing is offered as an attempt at a fair summary of what Seventh-day Adventism teaches on this point:

(1) The basis for decision in this judgment is obedience to the moral law.[12] The sinner, however, does not keep this in his own strength, but complies with its requirements through the power of the indwelling Christ.

10. Branson, *Drama of the Ages,* p. 316.
11. *Ibid.,* pp. 316ff.
12. ". . . a man's being reckoned guilty or innocent will depend en- tirely upon whether he has kept the whole law" (*ibid.,* p. 350).

(2) The believer is liable to commit sin after he is justified with respect to his past transgressions. In this case Christ is his Advocate, and will plead "the merits of His own atoning sacrifice in the sinner's behalf."

(3) The means by which the believer secures the advocacy of Christ for any given sin is confession of that sin:

> If every detail of a man's life is recorded in heaven, then his confessions are recorded there too, and, of course, the fact that Christ has forgiven his sins. The apostle Paul's comment may well apply here: 'Some men's sins are open beforehand, going before to judgment.' . . . When the name of a true child of God comes up in the judgment, the record will reveal that every sin has been confessed — and has been forgiven through the blood of Christ.[13]

(4) As for those who have sins remaining upon the books of record — that is, sins unrepented of and unforgiven — "their names will be blotted out of the book of life, and the record of their good deeds will be erased from the book of God's remembrance."[14]

This work of investigative judgment occupies the full period between October 22, 1844 and the Second Advent, which takes place when Christ comes forth from the heavenly holy of holies. Then, just as the final act of the Day of Atonement was the sending away into the wilderness of the second goat, Azael, laden with the sins of the people, so the antitypical Day of Atonement closes.

> Upon Satan, the instigator of sin, is rolled back his responsibility for having initiated and introduced iniquity into the universe. . . . Our Saviour then returns to the earth in glory, and it is *then* that Satan is cast into the bottomless pit, where he and his confederates in rebellion remain for the millennial thousand years of Revelation 20:1. Then at the end of the thousand years the wicked dead are raised to life, and together with the devil and his angels are cast into the lake of fire.[15]

13. *Questions on Doctrine*, pp. 441ff.
14. White, *The Great Controversy*, p. 483.
15. *Questions on Doctrine*, p. 444.

We proceed now to an evaluation of the distinctive views of Seventh-day Adventism on the doctrine of salvation. Obviously, we have much to do here with the significance of the Old Testament sanctuary services, for it is upon the position which the movement takes with respect to these that much of its case is founded. First, therefore, we will discuss the question of whether or not the Adventist construction is compatible with the teaching of the Old Testament as to the meaning of the sacrificial system.

THE ADVENTIST CONCEPTION OF THE SANCTUARY SERVICES

Concerning the sacrifices of the Old Testament, the Adventists say that they all pointed forward to Christ, but that "it took various sacrifices, or phases of the sacrificial work, to represent the all-inclusive work of Jesus as the great antitypical sacrifice for the redemption of a lost race."[16] This, to be sure, is substantially the position of orthodox Protestantism, and no exception need be taken to the general notion expressed by this quotation. It is when the Adventists begin to expound the meaning of the various sacrifices, however, and to relate them to the idea of the nature of Christ's atonement that the views which they express are peculiar to themselves, and demand close scrutiny. Particularly is this true of the distinctions which they draw among the several types of sacrifice, namely, the continual burnt offering, the daily sacrifice, and the yearly sacrifice offered on the Day of Atonement.

First, then, we take note of the discrimination which the Adventist scheme makes between the continual burnt offering and the daily sacrifice. It may be granted at once that there is a sense in which the burnt offering generically, which included but was not confined to the continual morning and evening sacrifice, was basic to the whole Mosaic ritual. Fairbairn, for example, remarks that to a considerable extent this offering combined in itself what belonged to the other sacrifices, and in a sense represented the whole sacrificial system.[17] He and others also observe that the altar of sacrifice itself was called "the altar of burnt offering." Nevertheless, there is serious question as to the validity of the Adventist construction that the

16. *Ibid.*, p. 357.
17. Patrick Fairbairn, *The Typology of Scripture* (New York: Funk and Wagnalls Company, 1900), II, 345.

"continual" was designed to represent *provided* atonement and the individual sacrifices *appropriated* atonement, the former representing the divine provision for men, the latter man's acceptance of this provision. This is so for the following reasons:

(1) The sacrifice of the whole burnt offering, to which class the "continual" belonged, contained, as did all the offerings, the element of expiation. *But the continual burnt offering was not primarily an expiatory transaction.* Rather, it was *par excellence* that sacrifice which symbolized consecration. Thus, while the continual burnt offering partook of those features which the animal sacrifices possessed in common, namely, the laying on of hands by the offerer, the slaying of the victim and the manipulation of the blood, the aspect which made it distinctive was its signifying the dedication of the offerer to the service of God. Of the continual morning and evening sacrifice, Fairbairn points out that it symbolized "what Israel should have been ever receiving from Jehovah as the God of the covenant, and what they, as children of the covenant, should ever have yielded to Him in return."[18] Therefore, while the morning and evening sacrifices did indeed symbolize "atonement provided," they symbolized to a greater extent the "sinner's response." That is to say, if any one feature was prominent in these offerings, it was that of the covenant people, as a people, consecrating itself to God in uninterrupted dedication, and its imploring of Him a gracious acceptance.

(2) The Adventists see in the other sacrifices brought by individuals and the congregation — burnt offerings, peace offerings, sin offerings, meal offerings, and trespass offerings — "the sinner's responsive offerings." These were "not a means of salvation but an evidence of faith," in that they were provided by the sinner and acknowledged as his substitute by the imposition of hands and confession of sin.

The difficulty with the Adventist construction here is in its attempt to force into a single mold a body of data which plainly does not permit of such treatment. For one thing, just as the whole burnt offerings of the continual sacrifice were congregationally provided, attesting to the fact that these offerings had congregational relevance, so in the case of a sin offering for the whole congregation the sacrifice was provided by it and confes-

18. *Ibid.*

sion of its sin made representatively through the elders (Lev. 4:13ff.). A sin offering for the whole congregation, then, was in every way as much an offering by and for Israel as a people as was the "continual." Again, while in several of the offerings other considerations were predominant — the "sinner's responsive offerings" may not be the worst possible way of describing these — the sin offering was to the idea of expiation what the whole burnt offering was to that of consecration. Indeed, the sin offering is the one type of sacrifice which is associated in Scripture specifically with the death of Christ for sinners (Heb. 13:11ff.). If then there is any differentiation to be allowed between offerings which signified "atonement provided" and the "sinner's response," the sin offering is by all means to be included in the former category. The Adventists' distinction between offerings which were "means of salvation" and others which were "an evidence of faith" requires careful qualification, but once again, if such terminology is to be permitted, "means of salvation" certainly is descriptive of the sin offering.

(3) The Adventists make something of the notion that whether or not he sought their benefits, the continual burnt offerings were offered on the sinner's behalf. But this is a misapprehension of the entire meaning of the Old Testament sacrifices. A discussion of the efficacy of these is not to be entered into here, but it may safely be denied that the sacrifices were intended for the benefit of those who did not appropriate them in faith. This was the case not only with the morning and evening sacrifices, but also with the other congregationally and individually provided offerings. The prophets whom God sent to the people of Israel gave a fair amount of time to disabusing them of the notion that He is pleased with sacrifices not accompanied by a broken and contrite heart.

Secondly, we must examine the interpretation which Seventh-day Adventism gives to the yearly Day of Atonement. This, of course, is of crucial importance to the theology of the movement, furnishing as it does the most important argument for the theory, distinctive with Adventism, of the two phases of the heavenly ministry of Christ. For several reasons this construction must be controverted:

(1) Adventism attaches considerable weight to the idea that the various sacrifices offered throughout the year were the

vehicle for "polluting the sanctuary." According to this view, the blood of the victim in some way "transferred" sins from the offerer to the holy places,[19] and these, in figure, remained there until they were "blotted out" on the Day of Atonement.

This interpretation, however, is demonstrably at odds with the teaching of the Old Testament. This is not to deny that there was some significance to the fact that the blood of certain offerings was brought into the sanctuary.[20] But the thought of the blood of sacrifice as being in any sense a means of transferring pollution is foreign to the Biblical usage; it should be evident to any reader of Holy Scripture that the pervasive meaning of the sprinkling of blood in the religion of the Old Testament was that of *cleansing* from the defilement of sin. The placing of blood on the horns of the altar of incense, or the sprinkling of it toward the veil before the most holy place did not, therefore, symbolize the transference of sins into the sanctuary; it symbolized rather the cleansing of the holy things from defilement caused by the people's iniquities.

(2) The Adventist view of the meaning of the Day of Atonement, in relation to the ordinary sacrifices, may be challenged. This interpretation depends to a large extent upon the foregoing estimate of the significance of the manipulation of the blood of the offerings within the holy place which, we judge, has been demonstrated to be unfeasible. It is true, of course, that in connection with the prescriptions in Leviticus 16 for the Day of Atonement a "cleansing of the sanctuary" by the blood of the offering is part of the ritual, and a part whose significance must

19. "As the sins of the people were anciently transferred, in figure, to the sanctuary by the blood of the sin offering, etc." — Ellen G. White, *The Story of Redemption* (Washington, D.C.: Review and Herald, 1947), p. 378.

20. S. H. Kellogg's remarks on this point are instructive. He says: "In that [the anointed priest] had a peculiar position of nearer access to God than others . . . his sin is regarded as having defiled the Holy Place itself; and in that Holy Place must Jehovah see atoning blood ere the priest's position before God can be reestablished. And the same principle required that also in the Holy Place must the blood be presented for the sin of the whole congregation. For Israel . . . was 'a kingdom of priests' . . . . Thus . . . their collective sin was regarded as defiling the Holy Place in which, through their representatives, the priests, they ideally ministered." S. H. Kellogg, *An Exposition of the Bible* (Hartford, Conn.: The S. S. Scranton Co., 1903), I, 271.

not be overlooked. Further, it seems clear that this service did constitute a reflection upon the inadequacy of the expiatory offerings made over the course of the year, and, in that it was to provide atonement for all the sins of the people, even those sins which had been confessed and forgiven through the medium of the other sacrifices came under its purview. The reason for this, however, lies in another direction from that which the teaching of Seventh-day Adventism supposes. It was not at all that the blood of the offerings "transferred" the sins into the sanctuary where they were blotted out on the Day of Atonement. Much less did this "cleansing" mean that the other offerings symbolized the faith of the believer in the sacrifice of Christ, whose blood is the means of the "transference" of the sins of the saints into the heavenly sanctuary to await final disposition during the antitypical Day of Atonement. The reason, rather, is that, as Fairbairn puts it,

> It was virtually implied [by the Day of Atonement] that the acts of expiation which were ever taking place throughout the year but imperfectly satisfied for the iniquities of the people, since the people were still kept outwardly at some distance from the immediate dwelling place of God, and could not even through their consecrated head be allowed to go within the veil. So that when a service was instituted with the view of giving a representation of complete admission to God's presence and fellowship, the mass of sin must again be brought into consideration, that it might be blotted out by a more perfect atonement.[21]

In the light of such an evaluation of the annual Day of Atonement we may best understand the expressions of Leviticus 16:16, 20.[22] For on that solemn occasion in the life of the covenant

21. Fairbairn, *op. cit.*, p. 337. See also G. F. Oehler, *Theology of the Old Testament* (New York: Funk and Wagnalls, 1885), p. 313. Note especially his remark that it was peculiar to the Mosaic system to accumulate acts of atonement for the express purpose of producing a consciousness of their own inadequacy.

22. "[The high priest] shall make an atonement for the holy place because of the uncleanness of the children of Israel . . . and so shall he do for the tabernacle of the congregation, that dwelleth among them in the midst of their uncleanness. . . . And when he hath made an end of reconciling the holy place, and the tabernacle of the congregation, he shall bring the live goat."

people, a single, all-comprehensive offering was made in their behalf. On that day the nation as a whole was called upon to "afflict itself" in recognition of its sins and its need for cleansing. And so pervasive was the corporate defilement of the people that even those things which they employed in the worship of God were envisioned as contracting a pollution for which atoning blood was necessary. One datum which Seventh-day Adventism might do well to consider in connection with its understanding of the meaning of the Day of Atonement is that *in addition to the sanctuary proper, the altar of burnt offering, from which the sins were allegedly "transferred" into the holy place by the sacrifices, was included in the cleansings* — see Leviticus 16:18-19. On the view of the Day of Atonement outlined above, that this should have been so is natural and proper; on the Adventist view it is difficult, if not impossible, of explanation.

(3) Thirdly, some notice should be taken of an aspect of the position of the Adventists on this subject which has attracted considerable attention from their critics. This is the theory respecting "Azazel," according to which this word, incorrectly translated "scapegoat" by the Authorized Version at Leviticus 16:8ff., represents Satan, the instigator of sin. Thus when the atonement, through the sacrifice of the goat upon which the lot fell "for the Lord" was completed, the live goat, upon whose head the sins of the people were in symbol transferred, was sent into the wilderness to die. He, therefore, was a type of the final retributive punishment of Satan for all the sins of the universe.

As might be expected, the Adventists have time and again been charged with making Satan the "sin bearer" and ultimately the saviour of sinners. They have repudiated this accusation, insisting that what is meant is that Satan is punished for, but in no sense atones for, the sins of the world.[23] The denomination, however, is without question in a difficult position here, for the implication can scarcely be avoided that if Satan indeed bears the penalty of "forgiven sins" the atonement of Christ is in some sense incomplete, and Satan a virtual "sin bearer" after all. Even if this point is not pressed to its logical conclusion, the fact

23. "Seventh-day Adventists repudiate *in toto* any idea, suggestion or implication that Satan is in any sense or degree our sin bearer. The thought is abhorrent to us and appallingly sacrilegious" (*Questions on Doctrine*, p. 400).

remains that the view of the atonement which comes to expression here is bizarre at best; further, there are several exegetical points which may be adduced to show that Adventism's position on "Azazel" is devoid of support from Scripture. For one thing, the idea that the goat which was not slain "did not provide any propitiation or make any vicarous atonement"[24] is quite wrong. This goat was definitely a part of the "sin offering," Leviticus 16:5 reading:

> And he shall take of the congregation of the children of Israel *two* kids of the goats for *a* sin offering, and one ram for a burnt offering.

Nor may we overlook the fact that according to verse 10 this goat was to be presented alive before the Lord "to make an atonement over him" or "for him." This signified, as Fairbairn remarks, that he "was the people's substitute in a process of absolution." The view that the two goats were employed in order to symbolize the expiation of sin and the removal of sin appears to be correct.[25] Again, even if it is allowed, as many non-Adventist writers do allow, that "Azazel" represents Satan, this is something other than to say that the *second goat* represents him. This goat "for Azazel," which was symbolically laden with the sins of the people and then led away into the wilderness, can on this supposition be taken to mean that he was sent as a witness to Satan that, in view of the transaction just completed in the holy of holies, he was now without power as the accuser of the people of God. That the goat "for" whom atonement was made and who was sent away should himself represent Satan is unthinkable; the Adventists have here indulged the precarious pastime of building a doctrine on a type. It is clear that they have misinterpreted the symbolism, and have thus introduced a strange element into the Biblical doctrine of salvation. If, therefore, their critics have drawn some inferences which are alarming indeed, the Adventists are at least partly to blame.

24. *Ibid.*, pp. 399f.
25. ". . . the sacrifice consisted of two, merely from the natural impossibility of otherwise giving a full representation of what was to be done; the one being designed more especially to exhibit the means, the other the effect, of the atonement" (Fairbairn, *op. cit.*, p. 338).

Turning now to the "heavenly sanctuary" view of Seventh-day Adventism, we remark first of all that this, insofar as it depends upon the above mentioned idea of the meaning of the Old Testament sacrifices, must be reckoned along with it to be incompatible with the facts available to us in the Scriptural account. That is to say, if the typical sanctuary services including the Day of Atonement, are to be viewed as a setting forth of the need for and the promise of a better sacrifice, there is no ground for the notion of a heavenly ministry of Christ in two phases, temporally separated, the one signifying intercession and the other judgment. Nevertheless, it is not necessary to controvert this teaching solely on the basis of inference; there are several points in the interpretation which the Adventists offer of certain New Testament passages which will not stand close scrutiny:

(1) The idea that the sins of the people were transferred into the typical sanctuary by the blood of certain sin offerings has been shown to be based upon a faulty conception of the significance of the Mosaic ritual. But the notion that under the New Testament the blood of Christ, answering to this type, transfers the sins of believers into the heavenly sanctuary, has the effect of preserving, with respect to His atoning work, those very features which made the Old Testament sacrifices imperfect. That is to say, these sacrifices contained within themselves the intimation of their own insufficiency; in the language of the epistle to the Hebrews, there was in them "a remembrance again of sin every year, for it is not possible that the blood of bulls and goats should take away sins" (Heb. 10:3-4). It follows, then, that to see a further work with reference to sins expiated by the blood of Christ as necessary to complete the work of atonement is to relegate the perfect, once-for-all sacrifice of the Son of God to the class of those shadowy things of which it was the fulfillment.

(2) The point is made by Branson that Hebrews 6:19-20[26] which, if taken to mean that Christ had at that time already entered the "most holy place" would be decisive against the view that he did so in 1844, refers to the entering of Christ within the

26. "Which we have as an anchor of the soul, both sure and stedfast, and which entereth into that within the veil; whither the forerunner is for us entered, even Jesus, made an high priest forever after the order of Melchizedek."

first veil, that is, the entrance door of the first room of the sanctuary. In his own words:

> It is apparent . . . that when the apostle declared that Christ, our High Priest, had entered 'within the veil' he meant He had entered the first apartment beyond the first, or entrance veil. He did not indicate He had gone within the second veil. Therefore, this statement of the apostle is in confirmation of the fact that when Christ ascended to heaven He passed into the first room of the sanctuary within the first veil, or entrance door, there to begin His priestly ministry in the heavenly temple.[27]

Concerning this, one is compelled to ask if it is not precarious to judge "apparent" this estimate of the high priestly ministry of Christ with nothing offered in support beyond the observation that "the sanctuary had two veils. In describing the earthly sanctuary . . . Hebrews 9:3 refers to the 'second veil'."[28] For one thing, Adventism seems here to have overlooked the fact that the word translated "veil" (*katapetasma*), though not used frequently in either the Greek New Testament or Septuagint, can indeed be employed without qualification to describe the curtain separating the two apartments of the sanctuary (see Lev. 24:3 LXX; Matt. 27:51 and parallels). Hence, to say the least, the contention that Hebrews 6:19-20 refers to the outer veil has not been demonstrated on purely philological grounds.

But further, even more important is the consideration that apart from the question of the sense in which we are to understand heaven as the reality of which the earthly sanctuary was the "shadow," the several passages in Hebrews which refer to the high priestly ministry of Christ give no indication whatever that the author of the Epistle held the notion that there was any manner of limitation of the work of Christ on behalf of His people. The entire thrust of the relevant passages is in the direction of the view that under the Mosaic system the priesthood was confined in its ministry to the first apartment (see 9:6), the people not being allowed to follow it even that far toward the

27. Branson, *Drama of the Ages*, p. 289.
28. *Ibid.*, p. 288.

presence of God, and that the high priest himself was permitted to enter only once annually into the most holy place (9:8). Thus the sanctuary service was a "figure for the time then present," transient and imperfect in that it anticipated Christ, a "high priest of good things to come," who "not by the blood of goats and calves, but by his own blood entered once into the holy place, having obtained eternal redemption for us."

If it is objected that this "holy place" which Christ entered refers to the outer apartment of the heavenly sanctuary, the further explication of the high priestly ministry in 9:24ff. should be reflected upon. For here Christ is said to have entered heaven itself, "now to appear in the presence of God for us," or "now to appear openly before the face of God." Is it not then to do violence to the language to see delineated here anything other than the teaching that Christ, by virtue of the dignity of His person and His atoning sacrifice, is entitled to complete and continual access to God on behalf of His people, a right which was foreshadowed but faintly by God's sufferance of the high priest under the Old Testament to enter the holiest once annually, and not even then without the veiling of a cloud of incense?

(3) Before we take leave of the subject of the "sanctuary position," it is necessary to discuss briefly the import of Hebrews 9:23, a verse which Adventism interprets as follows:

> On that day [of Atonement] the "iniquities of the children of Israel" were removed. . . . The antitype of that service, we believe, will be found in connection with Christ's ministry in the heavenly sanctuary, and this is apparent from Hebrews 9:23:
>
> "It was therefore necessary that the patterns of things in the heavens should be purified (*katharidzo*) with these; but the heavenly things themselves (shall be purified) with better sacrifices than these (that of the Lamb of God.)"[29]

It is recognized, of course, that this verse contains mysterious elements; there are, however, interpretations of the words which are satisfactory as far as they go. B. F. Westcott, for example,

29. *Questions on Doctrine,* p. 266.

gives an exposition of the passage which seems to meet the
requirements of the case as he writes:

> In what sense can it be said that the 'heavenly things'
> needed cleansing? . . . Even 'heavenly things,' so far as
> they embody the conditions of man's future life, contracted
> by the fall something which required cleansing.   Man is,
> according to the revelation in Scripture, so bound up with
> the whole finite order that the consequences of his actions
> extend through creation in some way which we are unable to
> define. . . . And conversely the effect of Christ's work
> extends throughout creation with reconciling, harmonizing
> power.[30]

A glance at the Adventist exegesis of this verse is in order. It
is evident that the movement regards the crucial point to be the
temporal force of the verb to be supplied in the second clause.
The writers of *Questions on Doctrine* feel justified in taking it
as future — "*shall be purified.*" The absence of reasons for
arriving at such a construction is surprising in view of the fact
that there is not the slightest indication in the clause itself, or
in the context, that a change is to be made from the preterit, in
which the whole argument has been cast up to this point, to the
future. This can be accounted for only by the fact that no
such evidence exists, other than the agreement of such a construction with the "sanctuary position" whose validity has
been presupposed.

THE INVESTIGATIVE JUDGMENT AND JUSTIFICATION BY FAITH

Many of the emphases of the Seventh-day Adventists with
respect to the doctrines of salvation are not peculiar to themselves, but reflect the historical controversies on the several
issues in question. The Adventists themselves, as they undertake to discuss "the divergent views classified under 'Calvinism'
and 'Arminianism' " in *Questions on Doctrine*,[31] show that
they are aware of this fact. They inform us here that the denomination is neither Calvinist nor totally Arminian in its theology, and
that they recognize the virtues of each. It may be remarked in
passing that for them the Arminian position, as they understand

---

30. B. F. Wescott, *The Epistle to the Hebrews* (London: Macmillan
and Co., 1920), pp. 272f.
31. Pp. 405.

it, appears to be that which is in accord with reason and with Scripture. To be sure, there are issues at stake here whose importance may not be minimized. Nevertheless, it is neither feasible nor necessary in the present discussion to deal once more with material which has received exhaustive treatment elsewhere. There are, however, certain points which in the Adventist scheme of things are distinctive, and the most important of these is its understanding of the doctrine of justification, that is, of the sinner's forgiveness and acceptance by a God who is of purer eyes than to behold iniquity. Evangelical theology rightly so-called grounds this in the perfect righteousness of Christ the Redeemer, which God graciously imputes to the believing sinner. No question of human effort or of human character comes under the purview of the doctrine of justification, strictly considered.[32] This, however, is not the view of Seventh-day Adventism. That is to say, when the question arises of what constitutes the sinner's title to heaven, this movement gives us to understand that it is his keeping of the commandments: his keeping of them through faith in Jesus Christ, to be sure, but his keeping of them none the less. The following from Branson makes misunderstanding impossible:

> A Christian who through faith in Jesus Christ has faithfully kept the law's requirements will be acquitted; there is no condemnation, for the law finds no fault in him.[33]

In some respects this is reminiscent of other views which have appeared from time to time in the history of the Christian church, views which have in their own way compromised the gracious character of salvation by introducing, at one point or another, the notion of human merit. But it appears that Adventism surpasses them all. Indeed, it outdoes Rome itself, which it closely resembles in its grounding of justification in an

---

32. These do appear, we hasten to add, in connection with the doctrine of sanctification, logically posterior to but inseparable from either justification or several other benefits of our redemption; without sanctification no man shall see the Lord. But justification is grounded in the righteousness of Christ and is received by faith alone; it is so that it might be by grace. See the chapters entitled "Justification" and "Sanctification" in John Murray, *Redemption Accomplished and Applied* (Grand Rapids: Wm. B. Eerdmans Publishing Co., 1955).

33. Branson, *Drama of the Ages*, p. 351.

"infused righteousness," for the Roman Church, realizing that, at least in most cases, perfection will not be attained in this life, has thoughtfully provided a purgatory in which venial sins may be suffered for and the necessary rectitude attained after death. Adventism, of course, is not perfectionistic in the sense that it is unaware that the believer is likely to transgress divine law, the keeping of which, through faith in Jesus Christ, is his hope of salvation. It quite forthrightly informs its adherents that they are likely to commit sins, which are recorded in heaven and come to the attention of Christ as He ministers in the most holy place, and assures them that their confessions are also noted, and forgiveness granted through the blood of Christ. But even this can scarcely engender much peace of conscience when it is remembered that the Adventist teaching on this point is that the confession, specifically, of every sin that the believer has committed is required if he is not to be lost. We have cited Mrs. White's dictum; Branson similarly remarks:

> If it is found that one has broken even a single precept, and this transgression is unconfessed, he will be dealt with just as if he had broken all ten.[34]

What question could be more appropriate here than "Who then, can be saved?" For if this is the "gospel," the sinner saved by grace is at no point in his Christian experience any better off than was the Martin Luther of Augustinian cloister days, whose difficulty was "not whether his sins were big or little, but whether they had been confessed," and who discovered, to his dismay, that "some of man's misdemeanors are not even recognized, let alone remembered."[35] The conclusion is inescapable, then, that the Adventist doctrine of salvation leads relentlessly to a kind of "justification by character." Indeed, the believer does not, in this system, keep the law in his own strength; the merit belongs to the indwelling Christ, by whose power the Christian keeps the commandments and thus, being acquitted in the "investigative judgment," is accounted worthy of eternal life. For this reason it is not accurate to say without qualification, as some have, that Seventh-day Adventism teaches that salvation is by keeping the law. But it must be evi-

---

34. *Ibid.*
35. R. Bainton, *Here I Stand* (Nashville: Abingdon Press, 1950), p. 55.

dent that there is little awareness in Adventism that the believer, as a matter of fact, offends in many ways, and neither does nor can perform all that is required of him; that he breaks God's law daily in thought, word and deed, and has, therefore, a need which surpasses that of the forgiveness of past sins and the power of the indwelling Christ for present victories. The note is not prominent in the teaching of this movement, if it is there at all, that what the sinner needs, and what Scripture offers him, is a Saviour who kept the law on his behalf, and whose perfect righteousness is imputed to him. Because the Adventists seem not to grasp this foundational truth, it must be concluded that although the movement may be unaware of it,[36] far from inculcating the glorious tidings that a man is justified by faith without the deeds of the law, the "sanctuary position" tends to a legalism as deadly, if not as explicit, as the Galatian Judaizers' own.

36. "[We believe] that salvation through Christ is by grace alone, through faith in His blood."

"[We believe] that man is justified by faith" (*Questions on Doctrine*, pp. 22f.)

CHAPTER SIX

SEVENTH-DAY ADVENTISM AND THE SABBATH

Inasmuch as one of the foundational doctrines of Seventh-day Adventism is its view of the Sabbath, no discussion of the theology of this movement can very well omit to give particular consideration to this subject. However, before this can be attempted, certain questions related to Adventism's view of the law of God in general require some discussion. In the present chapter, therefore, we shall consider first the position which the denomination takes on the subject of law, and then proceed to the question of the Sabbath, both in its bearing upon the matter of the day for Christian observance and as it affects Adventism's view of the church and salvation.

THE LAW OF GOD IN ADVENTISM

Point six of the denomination's "Statement of Fundamental Beliefs" reads:

> [We believe] that the will of God as it relates to moral conduct is comprehended in His law of ten commandments; that these are great moral, unchangeable precepts, binding upon all men, in every age.

While this particular doctrinal statement does not deal with other aspects of divine law, the standard Seventh-day Adventist position is that there is an important distinction between the Decalogue and the ceremonial law, which is considered to be "the sacrificial offerings, feast days, . . . the priesthood, — all that was typical of the sacrifice and ministry of Christ our Lord . . . ." This, but not the moral law of the Ten Commandments, "met its end on Calvary's cross."[1]

Concerning the civil laws of the Old Testament — "counsel on human relationships, civil judgments, health questions, and many other vital principles of faith and practice"[2] — it is difficult to

1. *Questions on Doctrine,* p. 130.
2. *Ibid.,* p. 622.

93

construct an absolutely clear picture of the Adventist view. Dietary matters seem to be in the foreground here, and the Adventists keep the laws concerning these which the Old Testament prescribes. But the reason for this is not that the law of Moses has a binding claim upon believers living under the present dispensation. It is rather because

> God, . . . long before there was a law of Moses . . . saw fit . . . to counsel His people against certain articles of diet . . . and since we are physically constituted in the same way as are the Jews and all other peoples, we believe that such things are not the best for us to use today.[3]

More on this point later. As far as the broad distinction which the Adventists draw between the moral and ceremonial aspects of the law of God is concerned, however, their view is not peculiar to themselves. The historic creeds of Christendom differentiate between the ritual legislation peculiar to the Mosaic economy, and the moral law, summarized in the Decalogue, which is of permanent and universal application. The Adventists themselves recognize that such is the case, and by way of proof cite a representative selection from the passages dealing with the subject found in the several Protestant creeds, and, for good measure, add quotations from the writings of "eminent men of various faiths," ranging from John Calvin to Billy Graham, whom they judge to be in agreement with them on this principle.[4]

Such an extended treatment as the Adventists give to the distinction between the moral and the ceremonial law would be quite unnecessary, of course, were it not for the fact that much of the criticism of their teaching takes issue with it at this very point. This is particularly the case with those works representing the view which, for want of a better term, might be described as modern Dispensationalism. The position taken by such is that the law of Moses included both the ceremonial system and the Decalogue; that the Mosaic law as a whole was fulfilled and done away with in Christ; that because the present age is the "Dispensation of Grace," to maintain that the Christian is in any sense bound by the Ten Commandments

3. *Ibid.*
4. See *ibid.*, pp. 121ff.

is "to impose the law system upon the heavenly people."[5]
For the Dispensationalist, those who hold that the Decalogue is
of perpetual obligation are chargeable with "legalism." Indeed,
one of the prominent exponents of this system places "amillennial-
ists" and the Seventh-day Adventists in the same category,
adding that "the Seventh-Dayists [sic] are more consistent and
logical legalists."[6]

Now it has been said at an earlier point in this study that
Seventh-day Adventism is legalistic. The reason for which this
is so, however, is not because it, together with the historic
Protestant creeds, regards the Ten Commandments as God's
standard of righteousness in all ages. It is rather because
Adventism, in spite of its protestations to the contrary, makes
the believer's character the ultimate ground of his acceptance
or rejection by God. On the narrow point of the standard of
righteousness, however, the Adventists are on solid ground in observing,

> The position maintained by Seventh-day Adventists
> regarding their relationship to the Decalogue, and their
> distinction between the moral and ceremonial law, is fully
> sustained by the leading creeds, articles of faith, and
> catechisms of historic Protestantism.[7]

It is not our purpose here to make excursion into the whole
subject of the relationship of law and grace, or to assess the
merits of Dispensationalist theology. But as the question of the
Sabbath now comes under consideration, the writer would indicate that he is unable to concur in those refutations of Seventh-
day Adventism's teachings based upon an appeal to the discontinuity between Israel and the church, to the restriction of
the application of the Decalogue to the people of God between
Moses and Christ, and such similar formulations. When the
Adventists affirm, that the moral law of the Ten Commandments
"is the standard of life and conduct for all men of all ages,"[8] and
that it has been neither changed nor abolished, they are only
affirming what Protestantism has historically confessed, and, what
is more important, happens to be Scripturally true.

5. L. S. Chafer, quoted in C. Feinberg, *Premillennialism or Amillennialism?* (Wheaton, Illinois: The Van Kampen Press, 1954), p. 261.

6. Feinberg, *Premillennialism or Amillennialism?*, p. 260.

7. *Questions on Doctrine*, pp. 133ff.

8. *Ibid.*, p. 23.

THE SABBATH DAY

Whenever mention is made of Seventh-day Adventism, the feature of this movement which comes most readily to mind in the popular thinking is the fact that its members worship on Saturday rather than on Sunday. The introduction of this distinctive practice, as has been shown, was through Captain Joseph Bates of New Bedford, Massachusetts, a Millerite follower who, having come under the influence of the Seventh Day Baptists, had accepted the principle that "the seventh day is the Sabbath." As this idea was worked out in post-Disappointment Adventism, however, it came to mean much more than the answer of one denomination to the question of the proper day for Christian observance. For as it was discussed in the setting of the Biblical prophecies and the sanctuary position, first by Edson, Bates and their colleagues, and later in connection with the "Spirit of prophecy," the question of the day to be kept as the Sabbath ceased to be simply a detail of Christian ethics; it became now a pivotal issue with an important application for the doctrines of salvation and of the church. It is for this reason that a treatment of Seventh-day Adventism's position on this point must deal not only with its view of the seventh day as such, but with the implications which this has for these other areas of concern. First of all, however, we take up the question of the observance of "Saturday."

The Seventh-day Sabbath

Although the question of the Sabbath is not without its complexities, the argument by which Seventh-day Adventism supports its view of Saturday observance is simple and cogent. Its position is that the moral law, which is of permanent obligation for all men, legislates the "time element" of the Sabbath, namely, the seventh day. Since there is not, indeed, could not be, a command to alter the requirements of the Decalogue, it follows that in the Christian dispensation, no less than in the ages from the creation of the world to the resurrection of Christ, "the seventh day is the Sabbath."[9]

9. See *Questions on Doctrine*, pp. 149ff.; Branson, *Drama of the Ages*, pp. 397ff.; Lickey, *op. cit.*, pp. 393ff. The subject is treated extensively in all Seventh-day Adventist doctrinal works.

In corroboration of this, the Adventists take account of the references both to the "Sabbath" and "the first day of the week" in the relevant New Testament passages. They find here that Jesus, during his early ministry, observed "Saturday" as the Sabbath, and spoke of himself as "Lord also of the Sabbath." As for "the first day of the week," this is mentioned in the New Testament some eleven times. But in none of the verses in which this term appears is there an injunction to observe Sunday. Further, the apostle Paul habitually preached the gospel on the Sabbath, showing thereby that it was his custom to keep this day holy. What of the reference to "the Lord's day" in Revelation 1:10? This is not, as popularly supposed, a description of the first but of the seventh day of the week. Branson asks, "What did the Apostle John call the Sabbath?" and answers, "I was in the Spirit on the Lord's day." Next, "Is Saturday, the seventh day of the week, the Lord's day?" The answer to this is, "The seventh day is the sabbath of the Lord thy God."[10]

The Adventists also emphasize the fact that the Sabbath is a memorial of creation; a memorial that "cannot be spiritualized away and does not expire with the lapse of time." There is nothing ceremonial about the Sabbath; that is, its significance does not lie in its foreshadowing of something that is to come:

> On the contrary, it has ever had a commemorative significance, for it points back to something already done — the creation of the world and the human race.[11]

Such a passage as Colossians 2:14-17, which speaks of the Sabbath days as being among the ordinances which Christ nailed to the cross, and Romans 14:5-6, in which the "regarding" or "not regarding" of one day above another is made a matter of individual option, are understood by the Adventists to have no reference to the weekly Sabbath of the Decalogue, but to various services and holy days which were observed in Old Testament times as shadows of the coming New Testament realities. Moreover, certain Jewish traditions respecting the Sabbath — the "traditions of men" which never had any validity, and various encumbrances imposed by rabbinical law — were

10. Branson, *Drama of the Ages*, p. 431.   See also Lickey, *op. cit.*, pp. 403ff.

11. *Questions on Doctrine*, p. 158.

all "swept away by the teaching of Christ. *But this involved only the appendages, not the Sabbath itself.*"[12]

The situation is, however, that most of Christendom does hold, and for long centuries has held, to the sacredness of the first day of the week. The Adventists recognize, of course, that this must be accounted for, and in explanation of this development turn to the history of the ancient church. Here they inform us, first, that at Rome, about the middle of the second century, it became customary for the Christians to observe Sunday as a church festival commemorating the resurrection of Christ. But this was *"supplementary to, not in lieu of, the Sabbath."*[13] Next, through such circumstances as "the influence of Mithraism and sun worship, the existence of the heathen festival Sunday, the rising anti-Jewish sentiment among Christians,"[14] and the fact that the Roman emperors found it politically expedient to unite all the religious elements of the empire, the gradual change was made from the Sabbath of God to Sunday. This was the fruit of apostasy in the church. Finally, in A.D. 321, Constantine passed the first "Sunday law," and not long afterward the Council of Laodicea changed the observance from the Sabbath to Sunday. The true Lord's Day thus became an ordinary working day, and, with the exception of certain remnant groups such as the Ethiopian church, this became the universal practice in Christendom. It was in such a context that Sabbatarian Adventism arose in the 1850's to recall the church to the observance of the law of God in its entirety.

The First-day Sabbath

As we now turn to consider the question of whether or not Holy Scripture warrants the change from the seventh to the first day as that which the people of God are to hallow, we are once again on ground which has been explored thoroughly in numerous other works. Nevertheless, several classes of argument at which the Seventh-day Adventists and their critics join issue require our attention here. First of all, there is the question of *the import of the fourth commandment of the Decalogue.* This is by all means the most telling point that the Adventists make

12. *Ibid.*, p. 160 (italics theirs).
13. *Ibid.*, p. 166 (italics theirs).
14. Lickey, *op. cit.*, p. 378.

in defending their view that the Commandments designate in specific terms the day which God's people are to sanctify and, moreover, assigns the reason for which the "seventh day" and no other is the Sabbath. "We," they say, "take the fourth commandment without emendations."

In general, those who have simultaneously affirmed the continuing obligation of the fourth commandment and its observance on the first day of the week in the Christian dispensation have dealt with its import in one of two ways. (This, of course, does not include those denominations, such as the Roman Catholic, who defend the change as having been made by the church in exercise of its legitimate prerogatives.) The first of these is the position that the fourth commandment, unlike the others, has a ceremonial as well as a moral feature. That is to say, writers of this class find in this commandment a moral principle (the keeping holy of one day in seven) rather closely interwoven with a temporary ritual element (the keeping of "Saturday"). According to this, the ceremonial aspect ceased, along with all the other Old Testament types, with the accomplishing of redemption by Christ. However, the moral element was preserved and the requirement of the commandment may be discharged by the keeping of the first day. The change, of course, was occasioned by the appropriateness of God's people signalizing the resurrection of Jesus Christ, by which the new creation was secured.[15]

The other view is that, as a matter of fact, the fourth commandment does not prescribe the particular day in the weekly cycle at all; that is to say, the commandment itself does not warrant the substitution of "Saturday" for "the seventh day." The proportion of six days of labor and one of rest is thus the entire point of this commandment; the particular day upon which rest from the week's labor is to be observed is not prescribed here but is to be determined by other considerations. This is substantially the view of Jonathan Edwards, followed by Daniel Wilson and others. Concerning the specific day of rest Edwards observes that the Jews, from the fourth commandment itself, could not have known which was the day to be observed. He says:

15. See Charles Hodge, *Systematic Theology* (New York: Scribner, Armstrong and Co., 1872), III, 205ff.

The fourth commandment does indeed suppose a particular day appointed; but it does not appoint any. It requires us to rest and keep holy a seventh day, one after
every six of labor, which particular day God either had or
should appoint. . . . But they [the Jews] never would
have known where the particular day would have fallen by
the fourth command. Indeed, the fourth command, as it
was spoken to the Jews, did refer to their Jewish Sabbath.
But that doth not prove, that the day was determined and
appointed by it. The precept . . . is to be taken generally
of a seventh day, such a seventh day as God should appoint,
or had appointed.[16]

Some form of the latter construction of the matter seems to
this writer to have the most in its favor. The main reason
for this judgment, negatively, is that to involve the Decalogue
in the ceremonial and transient is too high a price to pay in
the interest of refuting seventh-day Sabbatarianism. The Scriptures as a whole, in speaking of "the commandments" do not
suggest that there were certain elements in them which were of
ritual import only. And on the positive side, the Scriptural data
seem to favor the position that the proportion of six days of
labour and one of holy resting is indeed the element which lies
at the heart of the commandment. Fairbairn points out that even
in the Old Testament no special stress seems to have been laid on
the precise day, indeed, that so little depended upon the exact
day that on the occasion of renewing the institution of the
Sabbath during the wilderness journey the Lord seems to have
made the weekly series run from the first giving of the manna.[17]

The Adventists, to be sure, are not without their reply to this
position. "We dissent," they say, "from the position . . . that
moral significance attaches to the distinction of the 'six-and-one-
day' proportion principle — or merely one *unspecified* day in
seven as the Sabbath — but not to the keeping of the day desig-
nated in Scripture."[18]

But this falls short of meeting the argument that the "six and
one" principle is precisely the point of the fourth commandment.

16. *The Works of President Edwards* (New York: Leavitt and Allen,
n.d.), IV, 622f.
17. Fairbairn, *op. cit.*, II, 129.
18. *Questions on Doctrine,* p. 165.

For it is not contended that the day of rest is "unspecified" in the sense that the answer to the question of the day to be observed cannot be known by the hearer of the law. What is said is that other considerations besides the wording of the commandment provide this information.

The Adventists object further, however, that the significance of the commandment is violated by the keeping of the first day of the week as the one in seven. God, as they put it in their popular doctrinal works, has a "trademark," which is the seventh-day Sabbath. Lickey, for example, commenting on Genesis 1:31, 2:13 writes:

> On the seventh day of creation week He made His trademark. He made it *on* the seventh day, *out of* the seventh day, by *resting* on that day, *blessing* that day. This is the plain, unmistakable record of [the Bible].[19]

This "trademark," however, has been tampered with. This "tampering" is not the entire abolition of the Sabbath, nor the disruption of the seven-day cycle as the weekly division of time; it consists rather in the observance of Sunday.[20] Daniel 7:25, a verse which Adventist literature calls upon for some exceedingly hard work, is the proof text for this tampering. According to this construction, the little horn represents papal power which would "make a deliberate effort to change God's law, and in particular the time of the law. The fourth commandment is the only one dealing with time."[21]

But Adventism overstates its case at this point. While it is true enough — as more than a few writers of the "Sundaykeeping" viewpoint, in defending the perpetual obligation of the Sabbath have pointed out — that mankind has suffered numerous ill effects by flaunting this divine ordinance, the specific application which the Adventists make is unwarranted. All that is involved in the words of the commandment, namely,

19. Lickey, *op. cit.,* p. 407.

20. An illustration used frequently in Adventist literature is a picture of a man standing, hammer and chisel in hand, before the two tables of the law, which are engraved upon a marble wall. He has cut out "Sabbath" and the two instances of "seventh," which are lying broken on the floor. "Sunday" and "first" have been engraved in their places. See Lickey, *op. cit.,* p. 438.

21. Lickey, *op. cit.,* p. 441.

the keeping of the seventh day following six days of work after the Creator's own example, is fulfilled by the keeping of the first day. He who keeps Sunday holy is not seeking independence from God in so doing; he is not necessarily any less a "creationist" than he who keeps Saturday.

To regard the first day as the Christian Sabbath, however, while it is not at all to disparage the doctrine of creation, is also to take cognizance of the fact that the meaning of this commandment is not exhausted by this concept. The Exodus account of the Decalogue itself, which makes gratitude to him who brought Israel "out of the land of Egypt, out of the house of bondage" the motive for obedience, contains this note. But the rehearsal of the Decalogue, found in the book of Deuteronomy, goes even further, and in the fourth commandment changes the reason for the keeping of the Sabbath from the memorial of creation to a celebration of something quite different, something which has more to do with the doctrine of salvation than with that of creation:

> Six days shalt thou labour, and do all thy work: But the seventh day is the sabbath of the Lord thy God: in it thou shalt not do any work, thou, nor thy son, nor thy daughter, nor thy manservant, nor thy maidservant, nor thine ox, nor thine ass, nor any of thy cattle, nor thy stranger that is within thy gates: that thy manservant and thy maidservant may rest as well as thou. And remember that thou wast a servant in the land of Egypt, and that the Lord thy God brought thee out thence through a mighty hand and by a stretched out arm: therefore the Lord thy God commanded thee to keep the sabbath day (Deut. 5:13-15).

Thus, if the Adventists wish to take the position that this commandment has meaning only as it has reference to creation, they would be quite as justified in accusing Moses of tampering with "God's trademark" as they are in charging "Sunday-keepers" with doing so.

The Sabbath, then, is susceptible of a wider range of meaning than the Adventists allow it. It is employed in the Old Testament itself in what might be called a sacramental way, not only as the "seal" of God the Creator, but in the interest of calling the people's attention to the magnitude of the deliverance of which they had been the object — in a word, to their "redemption." There can, therefore, be no *a priori* objection to bringing the Sabbath into connection with a notion that goes beyond that of creation pure and simple; the Scriptures themselves do that in the passage referred to above.   Thus we are not surprised to find them ascribing elsewhere a significance to the Sabbath as a type of the rest which awaits the people of God (see Ps. 95, Heb. 4:1-11).

Our particular interest here, however, is the Sabbath law in relation to the Covenant of Grace, for it is at this point that the question of the change of day takes on its significance.   A cogent analysis of this aspect of the subject is given by Geerhardus Vos, who observes that while the Old Testament and the New have in common the fact that it is not by his own work but through Christ that man enters into rest, the two administrations of the Covenant differ in perspective.   The Old Covenant, in that it anticipated the performance of the Messianic work, reflected this by placing the days of labor first and the day of rest at the end of the weekly cycle.   Those who live under the New Covenant, however, looking back at the finished work of Christ, "first celebrate the rest in principle procured by Christ, although the Sabbath also still remains a sign looking forward to the final eschatological rest."[22]   Vos sees in the observance of the Sabbath by the Old Testament people of God a typifying of the work of redemption, yet future, and the coming to expression in their calendar of this feature of their life.   He continues, penetrating to the heart of the matter:

> The New Testament Church has no such typical function to perform, for the types have been fulfilled.   But it has a great historic event to commemorate, the performance of the work by Christ and the entrance of Him and of His people through Him upon the state of never ending rest. We do not sufficiently realize the profound sense the early church had of the epoch-making significance of the appearance, and especially of the resurrection, of the Messiah. The latter was to them nothing less than the bringing in of a new, the second, creation. And they felt that this ought

22. *Biblical Theology* (Grand Rapids: Wm. B. Eerdmans Publishing Co., 1948), p. 158.

to find expression in the placing of the Sabbath with reference to the other days of the week.[23]

On the basis of these considerations, we are warranted in
stating that there is nothing in the form of the fourth commandment of the Decalogue which would prevent a change of the
particular day which is to be kept as a weekly holy day. More
than this, it is entirely congenial to the Biblical notion of the
Sabbath for such a thing actually to have occurred. It is
necessary, however, since the Adventists make much of the idea
that there is "no shred of evidence for a new holy day or a
regular first-day church gathering,"[24] to weigh the evidence
which the New Testament affords as to the actual state of
affairs in the early church. Turning, then, to *the witness of the
New Testament,* we shall examine the three passages which
are crucial to this debate, namely, Acts 20:6-7, 1 Corinthians
16:2 and Revelation 1:10. The accounts in the Gospels which
refer to the post-resurrection appearances of Jesus to His
disciples on the first day of the week are, of course, important
and provide the foundational materials for what later became
the day for Christian observance. However, there is no particular argument over the fact that these appearances took place;
it is rather the significance of these first-day encounters of the
risen Lord with His followers that is called into question by
Adventism, and this is to be determined more by other considerations than from these passages taken by themselves.

Acts 20:6-7. At the outset, in order to establish "first-day sanctity" it is not necessary to take the position that the church began
to meet regularly on the first day of the week the Sunday
following Pentecost. It may well be that Jewish Christianity
in particular did not at first abandon the observance of the Old
Testament Sabbath any more than it came immediately to see
all the implications of the New Testament age with respect to
such things as the Passover, circumcision, dietary laws, and the
rest. In these cases, there was a considerable amount of over-

23. *Ibid.* Vos discusses the entire question of the Sabbath on pages
155ff. The present writer, for reasons noted above, would venture to
differ with him in his judgment that "there is a specifically Old Testament
feature in this commandment which no longer applies to us" (p. 159).
Vos recognizes, of course, that the general principle upon which the
sequence rests is unchanged.
24. Lickey, *op. cit.,* p. 434.

lapping of the usages of the Old Testament and the New, usages which the Apostles did not venture to challenge unless, as in the case of the attempt of the Judaizers to impose them upon Gentile converts, there was a threat to the very foundations of the gospel of free grace. It is not unlikely that Christianity did not become generally free from the old ways until the end of the Jewish nation with the destruction of Jerusalem and the temple, which occurred in A.D. 70.

We should expect, therefore, that the accounts of the life and worship of the early church would reveal, not so much by express command as by indirection, that such a change was taking place, and that with apostolic knowledge and approval. Moreover, such intimations would naturally be forthcoming first from areas at some distance from Palestine, where the church was so deeply involved with the most fanatical forms of Judaism. And such is the sort of instance that is found in this passage from the book of Acts. Interpreters have from the earliest times discovered in this passage that the Christians of Troas were accustomed to first-day observance at least by the the time of Paul's second missionary journey.

Needless to say, however, the Adventists dissent sharply from the traditional view of this passage. Lickey, for example, reasons in this manner:

(1) Luke, in the book of Acts, "recorded eighty-four Sabbath services [after Christ's ascension] and only one first-day meeting."[25]

(2) This meeting, in Troas was held on the first day of the week and at night. According to "Bible time," however, the first day of the week begins Saturday night at sundown. This meeting, therefore, must have been on Saturday night.

(3) According to Lickey:

> Paul, having preached, conversed and eaten found that day was breaking. His company had already set sail Saturday night. . . . Sunday morning the apostle walked nineteen miles across a point of land to Assos, where his company took him on board ship. Neither Paul nor any of the believers attached any sacredness to the first day of the week.[26]

25. Lickey, *op. cit.*, p. 430.
26. *Ibid.*

Lickey also points out that the "breaking of bread" (v. 7) does not signify the Lord's supper; "it is the common Bible expression to indicate partaking of food."

Several observations may be made about this interpretation of these data. In the first place, the observation that Acts records eighty-four Sabbath services and only one first-day service reflects such a cavalier approach to the facts that it is difficult to imagine that the Adventists seriously hold such a view. Certainly their writers cannot be unaware that these "Sabbath" services recorded in Acts were not Christian meetings for worship at all, but synagogue services at which Christian missionaries appeared in order to preach the gospel to the Jews and any others who may have been present. Nor, further can it have escaped their attention that there is no record in the inspired history of the apostolic church of the occurrence of even one Christian worship service on a Saturday. This, of course, is not to say that it is thereby proved that none such were held, but it is not without significance that the New Testament is completely silent as to whether or not they were.

Secondly, the Adventists are dogmatic beyond what the facts permit in their view of the time of the meeting recorded in Acts 20:7ff. It may very well be that Luke was employing Jewish categories of time, and that the meeting was held on Saturday after sundown, the "first day of the week." On the other hand, a good case can be made for the construction that Luke, himself a Gentile, was writing according to the usage of the Graeco-Roman world, and that this was in fact a Sunday evening service. Foakes-Jackson and Lake, commenting on the verse, remark, after careful examination of the historical and linguistic aspects of the problem, "It is hard to avoid the conclusion that the meeting in Troas was on Sunday, not Saturday, evening."[27]

A final decision on this point is perhaps not possible, nor does it matter tremendously as far as our present purposes are concerned. What is of importance is that the first day, whatever Luke may have meant by that word, is mentioned specifically as the occasion of a meeting for Christian worship by the entire believing community of Troas, and that this fact is stated in such a way ("On the first day of the week, when we had gathered

27. F. J. Foakes-Jackson and Kirsopp Lake: *The Beginnings of Christianity* (London: Macmillan and Co., 1933) IV, 255.

together. . . .") as to give the distinct impression that this was a customary practice. If the worship service of the church at Troas had been held regularly on the Jewish Sabbath, that is, on the day before "the first day of the week" whether by Jewish or by Roman reckoning, there would have been no reason why the apostle could not have appropriately taken leave of the company of believers at that time, and spent the following day in ministering to individuals or in proceeding by easy stages to Assos (v. 14) to take ship for Palestine.

Taking account of the other objections to the idea of "Sunday sacredness" which the Adventists, on the basis of this passage, urge, one may point out, first, that there is not much cogency to their argument as to the significance of the "breaking of bread." Commentators differ on this point; the Adventists may or may not be right. But even on the assumption that the term is not to be taken in the sense of "celebrate the Lord's Supper," this hardly precludes it having been observed at that meeting if, indeed, it was the consistent practice of the apostolic church to observe this sacrament weekly. Again, the objection that it would have been uncongenial to the proper observance of the sacred day for Paul to have travelled nineteen miles, if it be granted that Sunday morning was really the time in question, is likewise to be dismissed as having little weight. The vessel was due to leave port at a given hour; presumably the ship's master had not consulted Paul about the sailing schedule (it would be an unusual captain who would consult the convenience of his passengers — even of Adventist missionaries — on such matters). Luke and the other members of the party went on board at Troas; Paul, however, for what reasons we do not know, remained for some hours longer and proceeded overland to meet the ship at its next port of call. There is nothing on the action contemplated which would have been in violation of the Scriptural principles regarding the proper observance of the Sabbath, if, as seems doubtful, Sunday was the day on which the ship sailed.

I Corinthians 16:2. This passage makes incidental reference to "the first day of the week" in connection with a gathering of money from the gentile churches of Greece and Asia. This collection, to be made by Paul when he visited them on his way back to Palestine, was to be for the benefit of the impoverished

Christians of Jerusalem.   His instructions to the Corinthians are as follows:

> On the first day of every week, each of you is to put something aside and store it up, as he may prosper, so that contributions need not be made when I come (R.S.V.).

The Adventist construction of this passage follows the view accepted generally by modern interpreters up to the point at which the question of the significance of the "first day of the week" comes into focus. Even here, the contention that "this plan had no connection with a weekly collection at a church service . . . the money was to be laid aside at home"[28] would find support in many expositors of the passage, and, as a matter of fact, is probably correct. The Adventists, however, go on to infer from this verse that the arrangement mentioned was actually in the interest of seventh-day Sabbath sanctity:

> How simple and clear is the picture. A church member runs a small shop all week, let us say. Friday afternoon he closes early enough to prepare for the Sabbath. There is no time to figure accounts. But when the Sabbath is past, and the first day of the week comes, he is to check his net earnings and lay aside a proper sum, not at church, but at home.[29]

Such an argument has some degree of plausibility, of course. There is a certain logic to the idea that those engaged in mercantile pursuits would find the day following the Sabbath a convenient time for figuring accounts and setting aside their contributions for the Jerusalem poor. But a practice of this sort was in all probability no more characteristic of the small business-man of the first century than it is of such a one who is a church member in the twentieth, who would scarcely require a formal balancing of his books at the end of each business week in order to determine how much he ought to contribute, and this all the more since, as the Adventists are careful to point out, the passage in question does not speak of the regular, proportionate contributions to the local church, but extra offerings for a charitable cause. More than this, the mercantile class does not constitute

28. Lickey, *op. cit.*, p. 433.
29. *Ibid.*

more than a small proportion of the total community; their particular situation would not be the basis for a general rule. As far as the large majority of the membership of any given church was concerned there would be no reasonableness at all to such a procedure. As Van Baalen appropriately remarks, "Imagine an Adventist laying aside his gifts to the church on Sunday!"[30]

Hence, although this reference is very brief, and one must not emulate Adventism in finding more than the text warrants, it seems fair to judge that the most obvious interpretation is the correct one, namely, that the first day of the week, the day which the Christian community in the various cities to which such instructions were sent reserved in a particular manner for worship and service, was the day appointed for the additional spiritual exercise of setting funds aside in systematic fashion for the relief of the Christian poor.

Revelation 1:10a. This verse reads, "I was in the Spirit on the Lord's day." The Adventists are in agreement with most competent expositors of this passage in considering that John's allusion to "the Lord's day" is to an actual day of the week, and not to the "day of the Lord," the end of the world. They are, however, convinced that this reference is to Saturday, on the basis of a syllogism which goes as follows:

1. The Lord has a day — the Lord's day.
2. Jesus is Lord of the Sabbath day.
3. That Sabbath day is the seventh day.
4. Therefore the seventh day is the Lord's day.[31]

Much here, of course, depends on the way in which the Adventists construe Mark 2:28: "Therefore the Son of man is Lord also of the sabbath." This, in their view, is intended to teach that "Jesus is Lord and the Sabbath in His day," or, as Branson has it, "If . . . the Son of man is Lord of the Sabbath, the Sabbath must be the Lord's day."[32]

This type of treatment, however, does not stand a careful scrutiny of the passages concerned. The words of Jesus in Mark 2:28 do not have a primary bearing on the question of "the

30. J. K. Van Baalen, *The Chaos of Cults* (Grand Rapids: Wm. B. Eerdmans Publishing Co., 1956), p. 210.

31. Lickey, *op. cit.*, p. 415.

32. Branson, *op. cit.*, p. 418.

day." They are part of a context, according to which Jesus, having been criticised for permitting his disciples to satisfy their hunger by plucking and eating a few handfuls of ripened grain on the Sabbath, appeals to the example of David who, in certain circumstances, did something that might have been construed as a contravention of a divine ordinance. Jesus' concluding remarks to the Pharisees were:

> The sabbath was made for man and not man for the sabbath: Therefore the Son of man is Lord also of the sabbath.

The inference is warranted that Jesus is here claiming the sovereign right, as Messiah, to determine the true import of the fourth commandment. The point must not be pressed, but if these words speak at all of the modification of the time of observance of the Sabbath, such a modification is within the scope of Jesus' prerogative, as "Lord of the Sabbath."

The meaning of Revelation 1:10 is therefore to be determined by historical and linguistic considerations. John's use of this term, which is found nowhere else in Scripture and which was evidently even in his own lifetime becoming a more or less stereotyped expression in the Christian community for the day on which the Lord rose from the dead,[33] points to the conclusion that it was this day that he had in view. It is thus not a thing to be marvelled at that this passage has been understood almost universally to refer to "Sunday," and that it was this day that the exiled John was keeping when the command came to him to write the book of Revelation.

Before this phase of the discussion is concluded, something should be said with respect to *the testimony of the "Church Fathers."* Seventh-day Adventism is well aware of the unanimous verdict of "such men as Clement, Polycarp, Justin Martyr, Irenaeus and Tertullian," and their treatment of them, quite naturally, is marked by unmixed contempt. Lickey, for instance, remarks:

> Martin Luther speaks thus: 'When God's Word is by the Fathers expounded, construed and glossed, then, in my

33. See Ignatius, *Epistle to the Magnesians,* 9:1, also *The Epistle of Barnabas,* ch. 15.

judgment, it is even as when one strains milk through a
coal sack. . . .[34]

Doubtless there is much to be said for the unfavorable estimate which comes to expression in Luther's salty prose. It has,
as was noted earlier in this volume, long been a matter of some
amazement how far the church of Christ fell from the Christianity
of Holy Scripture so soon after the apostolic age, and this is
amply reflected in the writings of those who survived by only
a few decades the last of the apostles.

But on the other hand, not even the severest critic of the writings of the "Apostolic Fathers" ought to regard them as having
only the negative value of attesting to the effects of sin upon the
human intellect. For at their worst they are not without some
usefulness in providing the only available information concerning
the historical situation in the early post-apostolic church. Nor
should it be overlooked that such historical details as these
writings provide, details which, more often than not are present
only by way of incidental allusion, would have been far less
liable to confusion than would have been the case with matters
of dogmatic import. It is sadly true, for example, that there is a
sacramentalism far removed from the teaching of canonical
Scripture to be detected in Ignatius, who in his *Epistle to the
Ephesians* (20:5) spoke of "breaking one bread, which is the
medicine of immortality, the antidote that we should not die,
but live forever in Jesus Christ." But bad as this theology is,
it is incredible that there should have been no such usage as the
sacramental "breaking of bread" in the Christian church of the
period from which his letters come.

This, for all practical purposes, is the category in which references to "Sunday" observance in these and other writings of
those times belong. Such writers were not engaged in making
propaganda for the substitution of one day for another, and it is
impossible that they should have mentioned in these communications to their contemporaries a practice unknown in the
church. It may be added, further, that the change of a day of
observance is not something which would have early found its
way into the church. That is to say, if the apostle John had
been a seventh-day Sabbatarian, it is unlikely in the extreme that

34. Lickey, *op. cit.,* p. 439.

those among whom he was still a living memory would have abandoned that day and become keepers of the first day of the week.

It is objected, of course, that there are not many references in the earliest of the Fathers to Sunday worship. This is hardly surprising, in view of the fact that writings dating from the first and early second centuries of our era are scanty in the extreme. Further, the day of worship was evidently not the occasion of very much discussion in those times. Such references as exist, however, cannot be dismissed casually. Let us hear Ignatius on this subject, who was martyred in Rome between A.D. 110 and 117:

> If, then, those who lived in ancient ways attained a new hope, no longer keeping the sabbath but observing the Lord's Day, on which our life too rose through him and his death (which some deny) . . . . — *Magnesians* 9:1 (shorter version)

Passages of similar import are to be found in the *Didache* and the so-called *Epistle of Barnabas*. At later periods, of course, from which literary materials are more plentiful, the observance of the first day is seen to have solidly entrenched itself in the Christian world. So patent is this fact that even the Adventists concede that Constantine's edict in A.D. 321, "enforcing 'the venerable day of the sun' by rest from labor [was] designed to sustain and enforce already existing ecclesiastical legislation."[35] To be sure, an absolute uniformity is not found in these later writings, nor, as was the case with so many other Christian institutions, was the observance of Sunday untrammelled by practices foreign to the principles of Holy Scripture. But that the church at large, since the most ancient times, forsook the observance of the seventh day other than, in some cases, as a day of fasting, seems to be beyond dispute.

THE SABBATH, SALVATION AND THE CHURCH

For Seventh-day Adventism, the question of the day on which the Sabbath is to be observed is in a class by itself as a matter of doctrinal importance. Indeed, it is of such basic consequence that there is, perhaps, no real analogy between this and the

35. *Questions on Doctrine*, p. 168.

other differences which have traditionally divided the several denominations of Protestantism, at least so far as the Adventists are concerned. For in the view of this movement, the seventh-day Sabbath is the touchstone of submission to the revealed will of God, a decisive factor in judging whether a church is truly Christian, and, ultimately, whether or not the profession of Christianity by an individual is a genuine profession.

This circumstance came about as the result of the studies of the early Sabbatarian Adventists of the relationship of their newly discovered "sanctuary position" to the question of the Sabbath. Bates, it will be remembered, had originally been converted to the keeping of Saturday by the Seventh Day Baptists, whose view was that obedience to the Ten Commandments required the observance of that day. However, as the "sanctuary position" and the seventh-day Sabbath were brought into co-ordination, the early Adventists came to the position that Daniel 7 (which speaks of the little horn who "thinks to change times and laws") and Revelation 14:9-12 are to be conjoined. On this scheme the beast is the Papacy, and the change from God's appointed Sabbath to the first day is the badge of papal power, the "mark of the [papal] beast."[36]

Further implications of this position, all of which became a distinguishing feature of Seventh-day Adventism's message, were that the three angels in Revelation 14:6ff. have specific reference to the Adventist movement as a whole. Thus the message of the first angel — "Fear God and give glory to him; for the hour of his judgment is come. . . ." —saw the beginning of its fulfillment in the preaching of the Millerite movement, which heralded the beginning of the "investigative judgment." The second angel's message, heralding the fall of Babylon, with its climax in the call, "Come out of her, my people" (Rev. 18:4), was, as Froom remarks, "likewise initially sounded in 1843-1844."[37] The Adventists see in this a prophecy of the withdrawal of many of the Millerite followers from the Protestant churches during 1843-44, either voluntarily or by dismissal. Contemporary Adventists soften this with some such qualification as Froom makes:

36. Joseph Bates, quoted in Froom, *op. cit.*, p. 957.
37. Froom, *op. cit.*, p. 958.

> Their action [in withdrawing] was not against the host of godly individuals still in the various Protestant churches, but against their official attitudes and actions as a denominational rejection of the imminent second advent through prohibiting the holding or teaching of such views. From such they must separate. And separate they did . . . leaving the various communions and forming distinctive groups of their own.[38]

Nevertheless, official Protestantism, of whatever variety, if not "Babylon" is its "daughter church."

The third angel's message, threatening the outpouring of the wrath of God upon whomsoever should "worship the beast and his image, and receive his mark in his forehead, or in his hand," was seen by the Adventists logically to follow the other two. Those who heed this warning are described in this way: "Here is the patience of the saints: here are they that keep the commandments of God and the faith of Jesus." The "keeping of the commandments," of course, involves for Adventism the observing of the seventh-day Sabbath. Indeed, the fourth commandment occupies a position of such pre-eminence that it is itself "the seal of God" (Rev. 7:1ff.). Froom adduces the "Spirit of prophecy" writings by way of confirming this interpretation:

> This thought was similarly attested by Ellen White, who wrote, 'This seal is the Sabbath,' and described the most holy place in which was the ark (Revelation 11:19), containing the Ten Commandments, with a halo of light surrounding the fourth. Thus the Sabbath and the sanctuary became inseparably tied together.[39]

The "seal of God," then, is the seventh-day Sabbath; nor is the recognition of the specific character of the mark of the beast left to inference: it is "Sundaykeeping." Indeed, as things developed, it became evident that not only is the beast to be equated with Rome, having "Sundaykeeping" as its mark, but, more particularly:

> The two-horned beast power, or the United States, enforces (according to Rev. 13:16-17) under civil penalty

38. *Ibid.*, p. 783.
39. *Ibid.*, p. 958.

the mark of the leopard-like beast, or papal power. So stringent will the law be that one cannot buy or sell unless he accepts the papal mark.[40]

When one inquires as to how it may be determined that "Sundaykeeping" is the mark of the beast, Seventh-day Adventism is ready with the answer. It is that the Sabbath, God's trademark, was tampered with by man, in accordance with Daniel's prophecy that the Papacy would "think to change times and seasons" (Dan. 7:25). Now according to its own testimony,[41] the change was made by the authority of the Roman Catholic Church. In this way the Sunday institution replaced the seal of God, becoming in this way the sign of papal authority.

It is but a step from here to the conclusion of the matter. The message of the three angels results in the gathering of a "last-day, commandment-keeping church." These are they who recognize that "Babylon," spoken of in Revelation 17, is the Roman Church and "come out of her." Rome, being the "Mother of Harlots," has as daughters those other churches who hold to and advocate Rome's doctrine and practice. These too are part of the great apostasy.

The Seventh-day Adventist Church, then, is the "remnant church." She constitutes the remnant of the woman's seed (Rev. 12:17) "which keep the commandments of God and have the testimony of Jesus Christ," and against whom the dragon makes war.

Adventism insists, however, that it does not believe that salvation is impossible outside of itself; it is necessary, therefore, to take note of several reservations which it makes respecting the "remnant church." The first of these is that, while convinced that the prophecy of Revelation 12:17 points to themselves, they believe that true children of God are to be found elsewhere, and that "Sundaykeepers" in every church, not excluding

---

40. Lickey, op. cit., p. 558.

41. The Adventists cite numerous Catholic authorities to the effect that the change of the Sabbath from Saturday to Sunday was made by the authority of Rome. The Redemptorist Father T. Enright, for example, is quoted as writing: "The Bible says, 'Remember that thou keep holy the Sabbath day.' The Catholic Church says, 'No! By my divine power I abolish the Sabbath day and command you to keep holy the first day of the week.'" See Lickey, op. cit., p. 442.

the Roman, who are "living up to all the light God has given them" are "unquestionably saved." Again, the "mark of the beast" has not, as yet, been imposed upon anyone; none are condemned until they have had the light and have seen the obligation of the fourth commandment. Before the final hour of history, however, all men then living will be put to the test. All the true children of God will "join with [the Adventists] in giving obedience to this message, of which the seventh-day Sabbath is a basic part." Many at that time, however, will yield to the coercion of the church-dominated civil power, accede to "Sundaykeeping," and thus deny their faith.

To give a complete evaluation of this position would involve us in details of prophetic interpretation which perhaps no one, at this stage, is able to formulate with certainty. Some few observations may be made, however, about the teaching of Seventh-day Adventism on these subjects. These are as follows:

(1) The view of Adventism that the beast of Revelation is to be equated with papal Rome is, as every student of church history knows, a more or less classical Protestant opinion. The mathematics by which Adventism discovers the number 666 to refer to the pope is also, presumably, based on the work of others. The present writer does not concede the accuracy of this particularization; far less does he discern the United States of America in the lamblike beast of Revelation 13:11ff. It must be remembered, however, that prophecy is a complex study, and the book of Revelation in particular has been the hunting ground for exponents of all sorts of vagaries, some of whom have otherwise been competent exegetes.

(2) The Adventists' treatment of the question of the "mark of the beast" is an example of inexcusably unsound historical method. For the movement has here placed itself in the untenable position, with respect to the Sabbath, of taking the claims of Rome at face value. That is to say, Seventh-day Adventism sees in Rome at every other point nothing but fraud, deceit and oppression. We are amazed, therefore, to find that on this one, isolated datum Adventism accepts quite uncritically everything which Rome is pleased to claim for itself. Whence, we are constrained to ask, this sudden shift? How is it that the Redemptorist Father Enright goes unchallenged when he affirms that his

church changed the Decalogue? Why has "Babylon," Mother of Harlots, servant of the Father of Lies, at this point and at this point only become the pillar and ground of truth? The only possible answer to these questions is that it is to the advantage of Seventh-day Adventism's theory to grant Rome's construction. Needless to say, evangelical Protestantism, confronted with such claims, has not usually betrayed such a lack of a sense of history, and has taken the position that the change of day was by apostolic authority and occurred before any such institution as that of the Papacy existed.

(3) The concession Adventism makes that true Christians exist in other churches, and that such as "live up to the light God has given them" are saved, has been used by various of this movement's defenders in evangelical ranks to prove that it does not teach that members of other churches are lost. It is difficult to see what comfort is to be found here. The Adventists are actually not retreating at all from the implications of their "remnant church" position. They are not for a moment conceding that orthodox Baptists, Lutherans and Presbyterians are members of true churches: these are still daughters of Babylon. All they are saying is that there are individual exceptions to a general rule, and that though guilty of gross sin (the flaunting of the fourth commandment), these, because of ignorance of the truth, are spared the penalty which might otherwise be theirs. That is to say, evangelicals, although they are doing precisely the same thing that constitutes the marks of the beast, are excused, at present, from the condemnation which such a sin will eventually incur. This, it may be predicted, will not appeal to many as being a solid basis for Christian fellowship.

(4) The all-important "message of the three angels" is very obviously tied in with the sanctuary position and the Adventist view of the Sabbath, both of which, it is hoped, have been shown to be untenable. More than this, however, the whole method of Adventist procedure in the interpretation of prophecy finds illustration here. This method, as we have seen, has been in vogue in circles other than Seventh-day Adventism from time to time. By now, however, it has come to be almost universally regarded as misleading and dangerous. The prophetic Scriptures were not given to us for purposes resembling those of a matching game, in which the meaning of a text in, say, the book of Revelation

is to be determined by comparing it with an outline of church history and looking for correspondences. When such methods are resorted to, as has been proved time and again in the field of Biblical interpretation, the results are generally what the searchers had decided to find before they began the quest.

CHAPTER SEVEN

SEVENTH-DAY ADVENTISM AND CHRISTIAN CONDUCT

WHILE THE DENOMINATION'S DOCTRINE OF THE SABBATH SUR-
passes in importance and in notoriety any other single feature
of the life of the Seventh-day Adventist community, this is not
its only difference with the churches in the general Christian
tradition on the subject of Christian conduct. Another element,
to which brief mention has been made earlier in this volume, is
a sort of comprehensive prohibitionism. This is closely involved
with its "health-reform" position, expressed in the seventeenth
paragraph of Adventism's "Statement of Fundamental Beliefs."
This reads, in part, as follows:

> [We believe] that the followers of Christ should be a
> godly people, not adopting the unholy maxims or conform-
> ing to the unrighteous ways of the world; not loving its sin-
> ful pleasures or countenancing its follies. . . . Thus the
> followers of Christ will be led to abstain from all intox-
> icating drinks, tobacco and other narcotics, and to avoid
> every body- and soul-defiling habit and practice.

Other Adventist literature is not so general in specifying the
things which defile body and soul. Liquor and tobacco, of
course, are high on the list, but the denomination also proscribes,
coffee, tea and meats which the Old Testament classifies as
"unclean." Abstinence from all these is a requirement for church
membership; it is reasonable to assume that disciplinary action
would be taken against any adherents known to fall into the use
of such. The non-eating of all meats is popularly thought to be
a tenet of Seventh-day Adventism. In a sense this is correct;
many, if not most Adventists use no flesh foods, and ordinarily
none such are served in institutions operated by the church.
However, there is some liberty on this point. Mrs. White herself, although a vigorous champion of a meat-free diet, did not
make this a test of standing, and went so far as to say that
while meat is not the most wholesome of diets, she "would take
the position that meat should not be discarded by everyone.

Those who have feeble digestive organs can often use meat when they cannot eat vegetables, fruit or porridge."[1] Modern Adventism similarly deprecates, but does not condemn outright, the use of the "clean" meats, and some members find it possible conscientiously to eat these.[2]

Legislation of this sort, of course, raises a series of questions on the subject of the Christian life, and in particular on that of Christian liberty. In some respects, Seventh-day Adventism's position is not unique; numerous churches and groups regard it as their prerogative to require of their membership conformity in the area of things indifferent — that is, those things which, in themselves, are not, by Scripture, required of nor forbidden to the Christian man. This has always been something of a problem; the troubles in the early church which gave rise to Paul's discussions of the matter in his letters to Rome and Corinth have never quite died out, and throughout the centuries Christian writers have given their attention to the issues at stake.[3] There is, however, one aspect of the question which is, at least in modern times, fairly well peculiar to Seventh-day Adventism and which, therefore, warrants some discussion here. This is the denomination's view of the use of flesh foods which, under both pre-mosaic religion and ritual law were pronounced unclean. The position of Adventism on this subject is not always set forth as clearly as could be wished. *Questions on Doctrine*, for example, holds that the issue is one of health only, and quotes Mrs. White as follows:

> To us, the whole matter of unclean foods is primarily a question of health, for we believe that God is as truly the author of physical laws as He is the author of the moral law.[4]

1. Quoted in Lickey, *op. cit.*, p. 468.
2. See *Questions on Doctrine*, pp. 622ff.; Lickey, *op. cit.*, pp. 464ff. The literature is extensive, this subject having been a major preoccupation of Seventh-day Adventism since early days.
3. No more eloquent or more Scriptural discussion of this question exists, in the present writer's opinion, than chapter nineteen of the third book of Calvin's *Institutes*.
4. *Questions on Doctrine*, p. 624. It appears that early in her career as the organ of the "Spirit of prophecy" to the Seventh-day Adventists, Mrs. White became convinced that it was her calling to give counsels concerning physical health. There is, therefore, a significant proportion

Anyone who has read more widely in Adventist literature, however, will recognize that there is something more to their position than this. The following from Lickey is typical:

> Don't let anybody lead you to believe that Jesus Christ made hogs clean. A pigsty is just as filthy, and pork as unclean as ever. . . . Not only may man pay now (by contracting trichinosis) for eating swine's flesh, but there is also a future punishment (Read Isaiah 66:15-17).[5]

As far as the present writer is able to tell, the Adventist view is that although the ritual laws of the Old Testament concerning food did in fact come to an end as to their ceremonial import when the new age began, the physical defilement which caused such animals to be forbidden remains. That is to say, it would no longer be required of anyone who came into contact with such material that he perform the ablutions, etc., required for uncleanness. However, inasmuch as the prohibition of the flesh of such was primarily for sanitary reasons, their use for food continues to be dangerous to health and, consequently, morally wrong. It seems fair, therefore, to conclude that the Adventist position is not quite fully described in the summary account given in *Questions on Doctrine*:

> It is true that we refrain from eating certain articles . . . but *not* because the law of Moses has any binding claims

---

of her writings devoted to this subject. *Testimonies for the Church*, for example, have a number of passages in which she offers advice on healthful living, and such works as The *Ministry of Healing* deal at some length with the general principles of the prevention of illness and the care of the sick. Adventist literature in general, as might be expected, has preserved this emphasis and has given considerable attention to such questions. Further, the continuing interest of the denomination is attested by its support of numerous hospitals, clinics and rest homes in many countries, at which the principles enunciated by Mrs. White, especially her views on abstinence from flesh foods, are put into practice. In most cases, excellent surgical and medical care are also available. It may also be noted that in areas where there is a concentration of Adventist members there are to be found "health-food" stores, in which the faithful can find such dietary desiderata as whole-grain baked goods and soybean "beefsteak."

5. Lickey, *op. cit.*, p. 467.

upon us. Far from it. We stand fast in the liberty with which God has set us free.[6]

For the denomination does make the non-use of such articles a matter of conscientious scruple.

As we attempt to assess the Adventist position at this point, something should be said at the outset on the point of fact which Adventism adduces in support of its position. Not being a scientist, this writer does not presume to evaluate the details of questions for which laboratory procedures and clinical observations are required. It should be evident even to the layman, however, that while health considerations played a significant part in the various ritual laws of the Old Testament, not excluding the dietary, these were not the primary reasons for their imposition. Further, while certain of the "unclean" meats, especially if unskilfully handled and prepared, are more dangerous than some of the "clean" ones, the line of demarcation between the two is not so sharp as to make "unclean" and "dangerous," nor "clean" and "healthful" precise equivalents. Numerous ethnic groups have flourished on the flesh of such "unclean" animals as rabbit and camel. Horsemeat, while not popular everywhere, is also considered by some to be appetizing and nourishing, nor, as far as the writer knows, is its use attended with any greater amount of danger to health than is that of beef or lamb. As to flesh foods in general, when Adventism points out that antediluvian man, who was presumably vegetarian, lived far longer than the meat-eaters of more modern times,[7] it is guilty of a glaring *non-sequitur*: there are numerous individuals and several whole races who eat little or no meat, but the days of whose years are still threescore years and ten. Nor can vegetarians, such as many Adventists and all Theosophists, boast any substantially greater life span than their carnivorous neighbors.

But these matters are not our particular concern here. Our discussion must be confined to the Scriptural data, for Biblical Christianity is committed to the position that nothing is sinful as such which the Word of God permits. The important question, therefore, is not whether the eating of pork can be danger-

6. P. 623.
7. See Lickey, *op. cit.,* p. 466.

ous, but whether such restrictions as Seventh-day Adventism imposes upon its followers are in force in the New Testament age.

The most important of the relevant passages which should be weighed is one which the Adventists themselves allude to, namely, the account in Acts 10:9ff. of the vision of Peter at the home of Simon the tanner in Joppa. With respect to this they say:

> [The vision] does not teach that unclean animals are clean but that Gentiles as well as Jews may be cleansed by the gospel. In the vision Peter did not 'kill, and eat.' Coming out of the vision he 'doubted' what it meant. . . . The swine is not ceremonially unclean, but physically as unclean for food as ever it was in the days of Israel.[8]

Now there can be no doubt that in interpreting this symbolism as teaching that believing Gentiles are to be accepted into Christian fellowship *as Gentiles* the Adventists have understood the real point of the vision. Nevertheless, their contention that there are no implications here respecting dietary matters is not well taken. For one thing, it would be foreign to the analogy of Scripture for a principle to be taught by means of a command to do something inherently sinful. Peter, as the object of this revelation, could not have understood the voice from heaven to have meant anything other than that the animals in the "vessel" had been taken out of the class of that which defiles. The words, "What God hath cleansed, call thou not common" did, to be sure, have reference immediately to Cornelius and his household, and ultimately to the Gentile world, but there was another application which Peter could not have missed. It may well be doubted that it would have occurred to him that the thing symbolized had been cleansed but that the symbol itself was still defiled.

Further, it is worth noting that Peter himself understood this vision to have had a bearing upon the precise question of the admissibility of dietary usages hitherto forbidden. Upon his arrival at the house of Cornelius he is careful to explain to him how it was now possible for a Jew to "associate with or come unto a foreigner" (v. 28). Without question, this had reference to table fellowship with those who had no scruples concerning that which might be eaten. That this is not mere

8. Lickey, *op. cit.*, p. 467.

speculation is proved when we consider the accusation brought against Peter by the Jewish Christians of Judea because of this episode: "Thou wentest in to men uncircumcised *and didst eat with them*" (Acts 11:3). The point does not have to be labored that the household of the Roman Cornelius would have partaken of food which a Jew, even an uninstructed Jewish Christian of those times, would never have eaten. But Peter defends his action by recounting the details of his vision. It may be concluded, therefore, that Peter's "doubt" as to the meaning of it all was soon resolved.

There are numerous other passages in the New Testament which speak on this subject. Perhaps a reference to one or two of the more cogent of these may be made by way of concluding this discussion. The apostle Paul, in 1 Corinthians 10:25-27, instructs church members as follows:

> Whatsoever is sold in the shambles, that eat, asking no question for conscience sake: For the earth is the Lord's, and the fulness thereof. If any of them that believe not bid you to a feast, and ye be disposed to go; whatsoever is set before you, eat, asking no question for conscience sake.

Now the Gentile meat markets of first century Corinth were anything but "health-food" stores. The chances are that neither the market itself nor the carcasses which were brought there from the pagan temples where the sacrifices had been performed, could have met even the most lax of contemporary sanitary codes. And yet Paul told the Corinthians that the meat, as such (other aspects of the passage do not concern us here), could be partaken of in good conscience. Nor does he discriminate between kinds of meat: "Eat whatever is set before you," he says.

Another, and for our purposes perhaps more important passage is 1 Timothy 4:1-5, which reads:

> Now the Spirit speaketh expressly, that in the latter times some shall depart from the faith, giving heed to seducing spirits and doctrines of devils; . . . Forbidding to marry, and commanding to abstain from meats, which God hath created to be received with thanksgiving of them which believe and know the truth. For every creature of God is

good, and nothing to be refused, if it be received with
thanksgiving: For it is sanctified by the word of God and
prayer.

Concerning this counsel which Paul offered to Timothy, two
points relevant to our discussion may be noted. First of all, in
making the unqualified judgment that every creature of God
is good and nothing to be refused, the Apostle was assuredly not
inculcating anything that resembled vegetarianism. Neither was
he giving a hint that the ancient distinctions between clean and
unclean flesh foods was to be preserved, even on the basis of
health. The contrast between this sweeping permission by Paul
and the following from the "Spirit of prophecy" counsels is
instructive:

> "To eat largely of porridge would not insure health to
> the digestive organs." In other words [adds Lickey], per-
> sons forced perhaps temporarily to a soft, bland diet may
> find meat of the 'clean' animals to be helpful.[9]

But secondly, the Adventists would be well advised to examine
carefully the category in which Scripture places those who
make abstinence from meats a question of conscience. This is
not an innocuous thing at all; Paul does not hesitate to condemn
it as a departure from the faith, a "giving heed to seducing
spirits and doctrines of devils." How Adventism finds it possible
to reconcile such words with its good legislation, the present writer
will not venture to judge.

Now all this is not to say that the Christian faith has no
implications with respect to questions of physical health. The
sixth commandment of the Decalogue has long been understood
to have broad application to practices and habits which affect the
human constitution, and matters of diet are assuredly included
in these. Further, it may well be granted that there are some
individuals who are either physically or emotionally unable to
tolerate certain things good in themselves; to such, the use of
these would by no means be in the realm of things morally indifferent. Again, if a Christian thinks himself obliged to refrain
from the use of some articles, Holy Writ does not forbid him

9. Lickey, *op. cit.*, p. 468.

that privilege, so far as his personal practice is concerned. Paul's words are sufficiently explicit on this score:

> One believeth that he may eat all things; another, who is weak, eateth herbs. Let not him that eateth despise him that eateth not; and let not him which eateth not judge him that eateth: for God hath received him (Rom. 14:2f.).

The question, then, is not whether Adventists may forego the use of one thing or another; Scripture gives them every right to do this. The question is, rather, whether a church which professes to declare to men the will of God may take into its hands the prerogative of legislating on the advisability of eating or not eating, and, in the case of the "unclean" meats, make "not eating" a condition of membership. When it does so, it places itself in flagrant opposition to the plain teaching of the Word of God, and thus cannot but come under the condemnation of Him who "for freedom did set us free."

CHAPTER EIGHT

SEVENTH-DAY ADVENTISM AND EVANGELICAL FAITH

Traditionally, conservative Protestant churches and missionary societies have regarded Seventh-day Adventism as being at best a sub-Christian sect; virtually every treatment of present-day cults from an evangelical source has included a chapter on this movement. And with few exceptions, relationships between Adventist workers, home or foreign, and representatives of these other groups have been no better than those between such organizations and Jehovah's Witnesses, Mormons, and the like.

The reasons for the existence of this state of affairs have been both doctrinal and practical. The latter aspect of the problem is not our particular concern here. It may be remarked, however, that inasmuch as Seventh-day Adventism thinks of itself as the "remnant church," it, logically, foregoes cooperation in religious matters with other organizations, even at such a modest level as that of comity agreements respecting fields of labor. It is well that we hear Adventism's own words on this subject:

> As the Advent proclamation is described in Scripture prophecy, particularly as it is set forth in Revelation 14: 6-14, it is commissioned that this special message of the 'everlasting gospel,' which is to precede the coming of the Savior, shall be preached to 'every nation, and kindred, and tongue, and people.' This commission makes it impossible for us to restrict our witness to this phase of the gospel to any limited area, and impels us to call it to the attention of all peoples everywhere.[1]

Foreign missionaries in particular will not need to be reminded that Seventh-day Adventist workers have implemented this policy with unflagging zeal. To many evangelicals it has appeared that the Adventists have considered it their special calling to make "present truth" known at least as widely in fields occupied

---

1. *Questions on Doctrine,* p. 627.

by others as in territories unreached by the gospel. They have on numerous occasions entered areas where, by dint of much consecrated effort a Bible-believing community has come into existence, and by divers methods gained a following.

Obviously, such procedures will tend to gain for such a group anything but warmhearted acceptance from those who do not concur in its estimate of itself. Nor need anyone, doctrinally at odds with Seventh-day Adventism, who has been involved in the distressing situations which its practices have caused, feel that he should regret having a negative attitude toward this movement, provided he has expressed his hostility in a manner in keeping with Christian ethics. The meaning of Christian love is tragically misunderstood if it is held to require the exposing of those for whose spiritual welfare one is responsible to what he is constrained to judge to be false teaching.

But while the claim of any religious association that the kingdom of God is more or less coextensive with its own membership is as ludicrous as it is presumptuous, this in itself is not sufficient cause for disqualifying a denomination as a true church of Jesus Christ. It is well known that at least several fellowships within the ranks of evangelicalism are, in this respect, different from Seventh-day Adventism only in degree. And, wrong as Seventh-day Adventism is, taking into account its principles, churches which acknowledge that many true disciples of Christ exist in communions other than their own should not exercise themselves to persuade this group to change its ways. Do not they too — and rightly — endeavour to reach members of ecclesiastical organizations which they consider to be at the periphery or beyond the pale of true Christianity? Seventh-day Adventism cannot be itself and desist from "proselytizing." It is thus neither realistic nor helpful to the evangelical cause to approach the leadership of this movement and seek to extract promises not to infiltrate other churches or mission works. Seventh-day Adventism would not act according to conscience were it to do otherwise than seek to convert everyone, whether animist, Muslim or fundamentalist, to its version of "present truth." It is better, therefore, that Christian churches realize that they are in a no-holds-barred fight than that they labor under the illusion of a false peace. As is the case with any type of error, the only honest, and therefore

the only effective defence against the incursions of such a
movement is to inculcate better things.

But our particular interest here is in seeking to determine what
the attitude of evangelical Christianity should be toward the
doctrines of Seventh-day Adventism. Recent years have seen
much discussion of this question in the conservative Protestant world, and the positions taken have ranged from qualified
acceptance to unqualified condemnation. It would seem, however,
that for all that has been said and written on this subject, there
has been a general failure to come to terms with certain issues
which are basic. For one thing, it is neither new nor particularly
relevant to observe that there are many doctrines which Seventh-
day Adventism shares with Christian orthodoxy. That this is
true probably not even the most vigorous opponents of this
movement will deny. Plainly, Seventh-day Adventism is not
guilty of the Arianism (officially, at least) of the Jehovah's
Witnesses religion, the idealistic pantheism of Christian Science,
nor the skepticism of either the old or the new modernism.

However, for purposes of evaluating a religious movement it
is next to useless to advance such data as these. When the
question to be settled is that of whether the message of a
certain group is or is not the gospel of Christ, the answer cannot
be reached by the mathematical route — by computing the
points on which, formally, at least, it measures up to evangelical
doctrinal standards. Here not even ninety-nine per cent is
necessarily a passing grade. In all probability the Galatian
Judaizers, whose message the apostle Paul anathematized,
agreed with him on almost everything but the one issue of the
necessity of circumcision and the observance of sundry ceremonial practices for salvation. Wherefore, then, Paul's refusal
to admit their teaching as essentially Christian and to move the
teachers themselves into the group of those who are brethren in
Christ? Why should a bizarre idea or two cause such a flurry
of excitement and prevent his extending the right hand of fellowship? The reason is that for Paul the problem was not that
of the number of doctrines on which these people agreed with
Biblical Christianity, but that of whether the details on which they
disagreed, whether these details were few or many, were in
areas of truth so vital that their denial subverted the gospel of
the grace of God. And so it must be for those who would follow
in his train.

In similar vein, it is to miss the point to join issue on the question of whether or not Seventh-day Adventists are Christians, and to castigate those who oppose this movement for what, in effect, would be the crime of rejecting those whom God has accepted. It is fortunate for all concerned that absolute consistency is not the door of the Kingdom. Some of God's regenerate people, undoubtedly, hold membership in a wide range of extremely unsound religious associations, and that there are such in Seventh-day Adventism need not be questioned. To admit the existence of such an anomaly, however, is not to condone it. Nor should evangelical Christianity use this as an argument for making common cause with a group in which dangerous perversions of the faith once for all delivered to the saints are to be found.

Once again, as has been intimated in several places earlier in this volume, it is to be regretted that many critics of Seventh-day Adventism have denounced its "commandment-keeping" in such an undiscriminating fashion as to relegate much of Protestantism itself to the ranks of the legalists. Apologists for this movement are quite correct in pointing out that the creeds of Christendom have never shown anything but the friendliest spirit toward the Decalogue. To cite only one example, all ministers and elders of Presbyterian churches have, at the time of their ordination, solemnly affirmed their acceptance of a system of doctrine of which a prominent part is that justification is by faith alone and that the Ten Commandments are binding upon Christians as a rule of life. Those who oppose Seventh-day Adventism on such grounds, therefore, would do well to review the historical Protestant confessions of faith, and, in addition, consider that the greatest souls through whom it has pleased God to bless His church — the Reformers, the Puritans, Edwards, Whitefield, Spurgeon, and the rest — held principles which sound very much like some of those from which certain of Adventism's critics desire to be "free indeed." But it is never necessary to check legalism by affirming views which imply the opposite error of antinomianism.

What, then, of Seventh-day Adventism as a theological system? Is it a more or less consistent form of Biblical Christianity, or is it a serious corruption of the gospel? There are cogent reasons, it is to be feared, for which the latter is the case. Further, so vital to the entire system are those views which, by any sober appraisal of the situation, set Seventh-day Adventism over against what has been historically called evangelical Christianity that it is impossible that they could be modified without the movement losing much of its distinctive character. Paradoxically, the opinion for which this denomination is best known — its "seventh-day" position — is not necessarily inconsistent with evangelical belief. Protestants generally, of course, believe that seventh-day Sabbatarianism does not rest on solid Biblical or historical grounds, and they are right in so believing. But there seems to be no good reason for which this peculiarity, of itself, should be a greater bar to Christian fellowship than those other differences which have divided the evangelical world, differences which, while serious enough, have not ordinarily been sufficient reason for the various groups to refuse to recognize each other as essentially Christian. Again, while Seventh-day Adventism has been charged, and not unjustly, with holding serious Christological error (see Chapter Four), it would seem that with but slight effort it could purge itself of this; hardly anything more than the forthright acknowledgment that some of its prominent exponents have been mistaken on this point would be needed to clear things up here.

But when all this has been said, there remain at least two positions to which Adventism is committed which no amount of modification, indeed, which nothing short of complete abandonment, can make to comport with even the most impoverished variety of Biblical Christianity. One of these is its view of the "Spirit of prophecy," which involves it in the capital sin of according to other writings a dignity and authority which true Christianity must reserve for the Scriptures of the Old and New Testaments (see Chapter Two). It will not do to seek to exonerate Seventh-day Adventism at this point by insisting that it does so unintentionally, or to excuse it on the ground of confused thinking. The movement, after all, has had the better part of a century to recover from its confusion and to tell the world that while for it the writings of Mrs. White are those of a respected leader, they are, after all, merely human interpretations and subject to the same limitations as are, say, the works of Philip Melancthon for the Lutherans or those of Augustus Hopkins Strong for the Baptists. But it has not chosen to do so. The latest Seventh-day Adventist publications, no less than the earliest, affirm in unmistakable language that these are "inspired counsels from the Lord." If this is not adding to Scripture, it may well be wondered what this trespass, so strongly warned against in the closing pages of the last book of the Bible, can mean.

The other foundational doctrine of Seventh-day Adventism which an evangelical clear in his evangelicalism must regard as being in essence "another gospel" is the "sanctuary position" (see Chapter Five). It has, on occasion, been alleged that this is a bizarre teaching, and so it is. But it is far more. For not only does it attest to the thoroughly erroneous estimate that Seventh-day Adventism has of the meaning of the Old Testament sacrifices and of the nature of Christ's atonement, but it evinces a notion of the way of salvation which is considerably less than all of grace. And we have Paul's word for it that if it be so, it is not of grace at all.

It may be hoped, therefore, that evangelicalism's present situation, difficult as it is, will not become even more confused by the acknowledging of a system so riddled with deadly error as having part and lot with it. It may further be hoped that those of conservative Protestant persuasion who, having examined Seventh-day Adventism's teachings, think that there is nothing in its doctrines to prevent its being regarded as a true church of Christ, will look again.

SELECTED BIBLIOGRAPHY

Barnhouse, Donald G. "Are the Seventh-day Adventists Christians?" *Eternity*, VII (September, 1956), 6ff. This is probably the most important article to date representing a new approach to Adventism on the part of certain adherents of modern Dispensationalism.

Bear, James E. "The Bible and Modern Religions: The Seventh-day Adventists." *Interpretation,* X (January, 1956), 45f.

Bible Readings for the Home Circle. Mountain View, California: The Pacific Press Association, 1916. This is a popular Adventist book of devotions for the family. It also contains an oft-cited passage on Christ's taking a sinful human nature.

Black James. *New Forms of the Old Faith.* London: Thomas Nelson and Sons, 1948. The chapter on Seventh-day Adventism is characteristic of the general approach to the subject by contemporary liberal Protestantism.

Branson, W. H. *Drama of the Ages.* Washington, D. C.: Review and Herald, 1950.
———. *In Defense of the Faith.* Washington, D. C.: Review and Herald, 1933.
These works are popular presentations of the Seventh-day Adventist teachings. The former volume in particular has been circulated widely.

Canright, D. M. *Seventh-day Adventism Renounced.* Kalamazoo, Michigan, 1888. Canright's work is the first and best-known of a number of criticisms of the movement by former members.

Clark, Elmer T. *The Small Sects in America.* Nashville: The Cokesbury Press, 1937.

Cross, W. R. *The Burned-over District.* Ithaca, New York: Cornell University Press, 1950. This volume affords a fascinating historical study of revivalist phenomena, including Millerism, in 19th century New York and surrounding areas.

Fairbairn, Patrick. *The Typology of Scripture* (2 volumes). Edinburgh: T. & T. Clark, 1864.

Froom, Leroy E. *The Prophetic Faith of Our Fathers* (4 volumes). Washington, D. C.: Review and Herald, 1946-54. The first three volumes of this work consist of an exhaustive and generally accurate study of the history of prophetic interpretation from the early days of the Christian Church to modern times. The fourth volume is concerned with the rise of Millerism and the prophetic principles espoused by Seventh-day Adventism.

Laidlaw, John. *The Bible Doctrine of Man.* Edinburgh: T. & T. Clark, 1905. This is the best study available of the Biblical anthropology.

Lickey, Arthur E. *God Speaks to Modern Man*. Washington, D. C.: Review and Herald, 1952. This popular study has also appeared under the title *Highways to Truth*.

Nichol, Francis D. *Ellen G. White and Her Critics*. Washington, D. C.: Review and Herald, 1951. This is a defense of Mrs. White's character and teachings. It gives the opposite side of the question to studies such as that by Canright, and should be read in connection with such works.

————. *The Midnight Cry*. Washington, D. C.: Review and Herald, 1945. This is a study of the early Adventist movement and a definitive refutation of the legends of fanaticism, "ascension robes," etc., which have falsely been attributed to the Millerites.

Salmond, S. D. F. *The Christian Doctrine of Immortality*. Edinburgh: T. & T. Clark, 1897.

Seventh-day Adventists Answer Questions on Doctrine. Washington, D. C.: Review and Herald, 1957. This work promised to be a clarification of the denomination's doctrines; some predicted that it would contain retractions of the views which conservative Christians have generally regarded as being inconsistent with evangelical faith. Many reviewers, however, have found it to contain nothing particularly new or more clear than other Adventist works. In fact this book is not much more than a rewrite of other denominational apologetics.

Talbot, Louis T. *What's Wrong with Seventh-day Adventism?* Findlay, Ohio: Dunham Publishing Company, 1956. This is a brief study of the movement from the dispensational point of view. It finds the new approach by other adherents of this theological position unacceptable.

Van Baalen, J. K. *The Chaos of Cults*. Grand Rapids: Wm. B. Eerdmans Publishing Company, 1958 (2nd revised and enlarged edition). The chapter on Seventh-day Adventism represents the same general position as that taken by the writer of the present volume.

White, Ellen G. *The Desire of Ages*. Washington, D. C.: Review and Herald, 1950.

————. *The Great Controversy Between Christ and Satan*. Washington, D. C.: Review and Herald, 1950. This work, reprinted many times, is one of the more important source materials for the study of the Adventist movement's approach to the Biblical history and doctrine.

————. *Steps to Christ*. Washington, D. C.: Review and Herald, 1921.

————. *Testimonies for the Church* (9 volumes in 4). Mountain View, California: Pacific Press, 1882-1909.

White, William C. *Scriptural and Subject Index to the Writings of Mrs. Ellen G. White*. Mountain View, California: Pacific Press, 1926.

Wilson, Daniel. *The Lord's Day*. London: Charles J. Thynne, 1913.

Yearbook of the Seventh-day Adventist Denomination. Washington D. C.: Review and Herald (published annually).

INDEX

135

Dec. 19, 1975